TOWARDS A
BETTER UNDERSTANDING
OF HISTORY

by

BERNARD NORLING

UNIVERSITY OF NOTRE DAME PRESS

NOTRE DAME   LONDON

UNIVERSITY OF NOTRE DAME PRESS

Notre Dame, Indiana 46556

First Published   1960
Second Printing 1961
Third Printing   1962
Fourth Printing 1963
Fifth Printing   1964
Sixth Printing   1965
Seventh Printing 1967
Eighth Printing 1971

Library of Congress Catalog Card Number: 60-15676
Printed in the United States of America by
NAPCO Graphic Arts, Inc., Milwaukee, Wisconsin

FOREWORD

When many books have been written on a subject the author of still another one ought to explain the necessity of adding his contribution. This book was not written because there is a scarcity of works on historiography but because none of them seemed a wholly satisfactory introduction to the study of history. Many are written for graduate students, some are research manuals only, many are largely "philosophies" of history, and some, though directed to college freshmen, omit matters which seem to me important. One who is taking, for the first time, a serious survey course in American, European, or World history needs to know three things: why it is worth his time to study history at all, what is the best way to study and think about the subject, and how to do elementary historical research. I have endeavored to provide, between two covers, answers to not just one or two but to all of these questions.

Perhaps the commonest handicap under which a beginner labors is that he frequently does not understand why he should take history at all. I have never forgotten a particular student on Registration Day, requesting guidance as to which of several history courses to take but specifying that he "didn't want none of that far back junk." It has been my chief purpose to explain why some knowledge of "that far back junk" is relevant to twentieth century affairs: why no one can understand his own age without some knowledge of the past. Secondarily, I have tried to provide some insight into history's timeless problems, to discuss the commoner interpretations of history, and to suggest study techniques which (it is hoped) will make history more meaningful and interesting to most students. Finally, since many students enter college woefully unprepared to do the most elementary research I have included a discussion (Chapter Ten) of the reasons for doing a history term paper and the proper technique to be followed. The instructions relating to technique are elaborate and precise because they are directed to a particular course: the Survey of European History course at Notre Dame. Formal requirements at other institutions will not, of course, be identical with these, but I believe the chapter will be a satisfactory general guide for beginners' history research papers anywhere. This book has been written primarily for college freshmen but it is hoped that teachers of history and some students in secondary schools will also find it useful.

I am deeply grateful to Rev. Thomas T. McAvoy, C.S.C., formerly Head of the History Department at Notre Dame, who read the manuscript, made many helpful criticisms, and who has in this and other matters persistently encouraged and aided me for many years. I am also indebted to Dr. Ralph Weber of Marquette University and Professor Charles Poinsatte of St. Mary's College, with both of whom I discussed the contents of the book many times, and who read the manuscript and suggested numerous improvements in the original; and to my colleagues, Professors James Corbett and Walter Gray, for their corrections and comments. Any errors in the finished product are, of course, my own. Finally, my thanks are due to the University of Notre Dame for generous financial assistance which afforded me the opportunity to write at all.

BERNARD NORLING
University of Notre Dame

April 27, 1960

The destiny of those who resign themselves to being the playthings of history is seldom enviable.—Raymond Aron

TABLE OF CONTENTS

CHAPTER I

Why Study History at All?

Every Man a Historian — History sometimes seems the world's most unappreciated subject. Who has not heard the old lament, "Why do I have to study history? Who cares what happened centuries ago? I'm interested in the present, not the dead past." The trouble is that the person who feels this way has never tried to think seriously about history. Consequently, he does not understand its value or relevance to the present.

Whether he knows it or not every person is to some degree a historian because history is the study of the past and everyone has some sense of the past, even if only the recent past. The human mind habitually moves in familiar tracks. People constantly think of the past, argue in terms of it, and try to justify or discredit present modes by references to the past. Get a group of people together and let them talk about anything. Before many minutes have passed one begins to hear, "Now when I was a boy we did it this way . . ."; or, "They tried this when Smith was Governor. It didn't work then and it won't work now . . ."; and so on. Without being aware of it the speakers are really acting as amateur historians. What they are saying is, in effect, that experience is the guide to any kind of sensible action. Now history is simply accumulated experience. It is invoked constantly and unconsciously by every person every day. Every farmer, sailor, doctor, lawyer, engineer, teacher, judge, or politician habitually calls on his memory or on written records of past events and experiences that are relevant to his work. Men in all these professions make mistakes, of course, but they would surely make more and far worse ones if they assumed that every problem they faced was unique and had no counterpart in anything that had gone before.

We are all historically minded, too, in that our thoughts and feelings are bound to past generations. A consciousness of a common past and common traditions is the most basic thing that knits together the members of any group, be it a family, a church, a nation, or some other. Who is so dead in soul that he is not thrilled by reading of heroic episodes in his nation's past? Who is not moved by accounts of the martyrdom of someone of his own religious faith? How would a whole profession, the genealogists, make a living if it did not delight people to discover that they are descended from William the Conqueror, John Gutenberg, or someone who landed at Plymouth Rock?

Each city, county, or district cherishes its own past in the same way as an individual. If this past is to be preserved it has to be written down. The habit of keeping records and thereby storing up the accumulated knowledge and wisdom of many generations is one of the obvious marks distinguishing man from the rest of the animal kingdom. Consequently, there are national, state, and local historical societies and museums; written histories of virtually every state, city, district, institution, church, and ethnic group; and of every intellectual, political, economic, or social movement in the land. One cannot drive far in any direction without encountering markers bearing the information that here is the oldest Presbyterian church north of the Missouri river, there the site of a battle in some Indian war, or there the place where West Virginia's state constitution was written.

Understanding the Present — It is a truism that one cannot understand the present unless he knows "what made it what it is." Anyone who respects the truth will want to acquire fairly extensive, accurate information about the past in order that he may judge from real knowledge rather than ignorance or prejudice. This is particularly true of a college or university student since he is pursuing higher education in order to become intellectually mature: clear in thought and fair in judgment. Consider an example. Jones is known to have strong opinions on a certain subject. A shrewd observer will not simply assume that Jones has come to his conclusions by a process of pure reason. He will want to know what sort of a person Jones is, what his past life has been like, and what are his ideas on other subjects: in a word, "how he got this way."

The study of history is merely the application of this common sense principle to a broader field. Every institution, idea, or practice of the present has been formed by the past and will influence the future. If one cannot understand *a person* without some knowledge of his antecedents and background how can one expect to understand modern political, social, or religious institutions (whose span of existence is not one lifetime but many centuries) without studying their past history?

Many thoughtless people talk and act as if the mid-twentieth century Western world of democracy, refrigerators, automobiles, air conditioning, and television represents mankind's natural, normal mode of life. They accept it all without question and seldom think about times past when none of these things existed — or even about much of the present day world where they still do not exist. This comfortable, externally splendid civilization, which is almost flippantly taken for granted, is really an amalgam of innumerable ideas, forces, movements, inventions, and practices lying hundreds and even thousands of years in the past. A few of these elements are Greek thought, Roman law, Christianity, Renaissance art, sixteenth and seventeenth century scientific conceptions, eighteenth century rationalism, French Revolutionary principles, the Industrial Revolution, and the political habits of the English people. Twentieth century society in the West is not one of these forces or the sum total of all of them: it is the result of an unstable fusion of all of them, for they are not all completely reconcilable among themselves. The proportionate influence of each varies from one country to another and from one generation to another. A history course deals with each part of this mosaic in turn. At the end the diligent and thoughtful student sees the complete picture.

Much that is said and done in the world is impossible to understand without some knowledge of history. How often one hears prominent clergymen, politicians, and other public figures assert that we are all heirs of the Christian tradition; that our civilization has been molded by Christian ideals; and that it is necessary for us to defend these. If this be true, surely a reasonable man will wish to learn something about these ideals and this tradition. At once difficulties arise. The first one is that there is not one Christian church but many different ones; and these are in striking disagreement about many of the ideals. Frequently these churches become involved in conflicts with civil governments which are supposed to be guided by the same Christian traditions as the churches themselves. From one quarter comes declarations that the true Christian spirit is to suffer blows meekly and turn the other cheek, and that, therefore, Christian countries ought to stop building such things as A-bombs and destroy those that they already possess. From another comes the reply that the very existence of Christian civilization depends upon maintaining a supply of these frightful weapons; that without them the Christian countries would soon be conquered by the communist states and Christianity systematically proscribed thereafter. Periodically some prestigious person informs us that Christian theology has been rendered obsolete by scientific discoveries but that it is desirable to retain the Christian ethical code. Other voices at once reply that this is the height of absurdity — comparable to trying to chop down the trunk of a tree while keeping the limbs aloft. Finally, there are plainly many prominent and able people in the "Christian" part of the world who show, by their daily actions, that this "Christian tradition" means nothing to them.

A thoughtful student will find this state of affairs confusing. If he is ever going to have any accurate knowledge of what this "Christian tradition" is, let alone whether it is worth cherishing and defending, he is going to have to study the history of Christianity. After commencing this pursuit he soon discovers that the life and words of Christ are just the beginning. One must also learn something of the history and traditions of the ancient Jews; something about the condition of the Roman Empire in Christ's time and after; something about the development of Christian doctrine and institutions. Before long our student is immersed in a sea of popes, councils, heresies, conflicts between popes and kings, missionary efforts, disputes about the dividing line between the things of this world and the things of the next, schisms, reform efforts, saints, scoundrels, inquisitions, Protestant revolts, religious wars, quarrels between ecclesiastics and scientists, and the rise of such modern ideologies as Communism and Nazism which have sought to destroy Christianity entirely. He discovers that through the centuries Christianity has fought some of its opponents implacably; that in other cases there has been a good deal of compromise, or even general acceptance of what was once regarded as unacceptable; that there has been wide variation between the Catholic and Protestant branches of Christianity in these respects; and that there has even been considerable variation among the different Protestant denominations.

At the end of his endeavors our student may well find himself more puzzled than he was at the beginning. If so, this is not surprising for the acquisition of knowledge raises more questions than it ever settles. But whatever his state of mind, he will now understand what is meant when reference is made to Christian traditions or ideals. Moreover, he will know why these phrases have come to mean different things to different persons and groups.

The foregoing discussion concerned a broad, general area of history. Let us now consider a more restricted case, the modern Middle East. To the observer who knows no history this part of

the world often appears to be a vast outdoor lunatic asylum run by
rival committees of inmates. News from there seems a monotonous
chronicle of revolutionary plotting, street riots, assassinations, com-
petition in inflammatory sloganeering, grotesque demagoguery,
Russo-American rivalry, and an absurd vendetta between the Arab
states and Israel. If one studies the recent history of this part of
the earth, however, he will discover what lies behind all this.

In the course of the First World War British agents made vague
promises of large sections of the Middle East to two different and
antagonistic groups of Arabs. Meantime the British Government in
London made a secret agreement with France to divide the whole
area into two spheres of influence, one English and the other
French. Then in 1917 Palestine was promised to the Jews as a
National Home. There was no possible way to reconcile all these
pledges and the corresponding claims that arose from them.

With the development of Arab nationalism in the last generation
most Arabs have become hostile to Western nations. They consider
that the English Government dealt with them dishonestly. Furthermore, they wish to be rid of the tutelage of all colonial powers and
to manage their own affairs. Finally, they bitterly resent the fact
that the English, backed by the Americans, refused to admit the
bulk of European Jewish refugees into their own lands but instead
settled them in Palestine, an area held by Arabs since the Crusades.
The Arabs know from the brief wars of 1948 and 1956 that the new
state of Israel is much more powerful than themselves, militarily
and technologically. They fear that Israel will seek to expand her
borders at their expense.

The situation is further complicated by the fact that the Near
East contains the world's richest known oil reserves. Western Europe
needs this oil. Russia does not need it but could score impressive-
ly in the Cold War if she could prevent Western European nations
from getting it. The Arabs themselves face several dilemmas. Their
nationalist fervor causes them to dislike the West, yet they need the
income derived from the sale of oil, and Western countries are their
best customers. Worse, the Arabs lack the necessary trained personnel to run the oilfields themselves. Hence they have to depend upon
unpopular Europeans and Americans to help them exploit their
own natural resources. The final twist in this snarl is the consideration that in all the Near Eastern countries there is a gaping gulf
between the small, rich ruling class and the penniless masses who
yearn for a higher standard of living. The latter are the element

most easily swayed by emotional nationalist appeals. Demagogues have arisen whose power is based on their popularity with these masses. Some of these "strong men" try to gain as much as they can for their countries by playing off Russia and the West against each other. Because of the great wealth and strategic location of the Middle East neither Russia nor the West is willing to see it dominated by the other. Each consistently tries to extend its own influence in the area and to blunt the designs of the other. It is all this past history, compounded by present passions, that has made the Middle East a seething cauldron. Yet without some knowledge of these matters how could anyone hope really to understand what he reads about the Middle East in the newspapers, let alone to prescribe any remedies for its ills?

Avoid the Mistakes of the Past — One of the greatest values of history is that it enables us to learn not from our own experience alone but from the experience of the past. To portray the mistakes of other ages is equivalent to putting a lighthouse on a rocky shore. To this the objection is always raised that humanity never sees the light: that men learn nothing from history. The complaint is pointless. The lessons are there to be learned, for the past teaches certain things quite definitely. It teaches, for example, that the persistence of unbearable abuses eventually brings revolt. It teaches that a class, like the nobility of eighteenth century France, which enjoys extensive privileges but no longer performs socially useful services, will not be suffered to last indefinitely. It teaches that the exercise of unchecked power for a long period of time invariably corrupts the wielder of that power. To say that people do not learn these lessons is tantamount to saying that they are too stupid or heedless to learn them, for the lessons themselves are clear. If the future of humanity is to be bright men in the mass will have to learn more about the mistakes of the past and be more resolute to avoid repeating them. It is one of the grimmest facts of our age that the weapons devised by modern science and industry have made the penalties for "mistakes" incomparably heavier than in the past.

History Is Necessary for Intelligent Citizenship — The preceding considerations have particular application for citizens in a democracy. Perhaps under absolute monarchy or dictatorship it is enough if the leaders are wise but democracy assumes that the ordinary man is sufficiently informed, sensible, and public spirited to govern himself and his fellows responsibly. This means, in practice, that he must support reasonable, realistic policies; that he must be able to distinguish the theoretically desirable from the practically possible; that he must be able to see through phony "solutions" to knotty problems; that he must be intelligent enough to avoid being duped by political tricksters and scoundrels. Where does one acquire such acumen? Unless he spends his life in the practice of statecraft he will have to get it from reading about past statecraft: history. Significantly, historians used to present their books for the education of princes and kings. They hoped that their royal readers would thereby learn what statesmanship was, what problems men and governments had repeatedly faced in the past, what solutions to those problems had been attempted, and what had been the results of those efforts. In a democratic society every citizen should seek such knowledge. The twentieth century is torn by fierce ideological wars. Their outcome will determine the character of civilization for generations or centuries to come. It is by no means certain that democracy will triumph in these titanic conflicts, but its citizens can markedly improve its chances if they make it their business to study the origins, nature, and ideals of their own society and of its foes.

Consider two important questions which ought to be the concern of every American: dictatorship and inflation. The manner in which inflation is ultimately dealt with will mean much to every living citizen of the United States. Now who is better equipped to think and act sensibly about this question: the person who has read extensively in the history of ancient Rome and modern Europe and who is thus familiar with the causes, course, and results of the greatest currency inflation of ancient times and the terrible inflations of twentieth century Germany, Austria, and Hungary; or the person who knows nothing of these matters because he is "modern minded" and "interested in the future" — not in "ancient history"?

Consider dictatorship. Not all dictatorships are the same: not all dictators abuse their power or their subjects: and in any case the possibility of a dictator overturning American democracy appears happily remote. However, dictators have frequently arisen in democratic societies in the past and, once in power, there is always the distinct possibility that they will misuse their power. Hence the proposition has relevance for every citizen who prizes democracy. Now aspiring dictators have a number of common features. In nearly all cases a man or clique seeking absolute rule tries to oversimplify some pressing problem and present it in vivid, emotional terms. He appeals to popular prejudices, flatters his intended subjects, blames most current troubles on some unpopular person or group, and promises a quick, painless solution to all difficulties if only the listener will have faith in him! Anyone who knows much history is familiar with this pattern for he has read of it many times. Thus he is more apt to recognize some incipient totalitarian movement for what it is than is the "modern minded" man who judges everything in terms of present appearances. In the much quoted words of the philosopher Santayana, "A nation that does not know history is fated to repeat it."

The value of history in a democratic society is not confined to helping ward off its enemies or providing guidance for the solution of its domestic problems. A spirit of moderation and compromise has to pervade the political life of a nation if democracy is to thrive in it. The study of history certainly ought to induce moderation in expectations. All nations and peoples of which history has record have known trials, troubles, suffering, tyranny, and injustice. We ought not to lapse into despondency but to bear up bravely if we, too, suffer some of these misfortunes. Moreover we ought to be realistic enough to realize that it is quite unlikely that we will escape all such tribulations. In short, history should teach us to be more adult.

History lends perspective, too, and helps people avoid ignorant or shortsighted judgments. Issues, elections, wars, which once seemed of overwhelming importance are seen after the passage of years to have been of little consequence. Thus to know history ought to make one less apt to be emotionally stampeded about some "crisis" in his own time. It has been well said that

> The . . . essential service of history is to restore to man, absorbed in his little concerns of the moment, a sense of due proportion, of the vastness of time, of the slowness of progress, of the transitoriness of so much that is eternal in its own conceit.[1]

Appreciation of Other Peoples and Cultures — Consider how much bitterness and intolerance, how much stupidity in opinion and judgment, is due to simple ignorance. How prone we all are to label other peoples as queer, stupid, or irrational because they do not think and act as we do. And most damning — how much of this could be moderated if we only took the trouble to learn more about others and how they got the way they are. History can be a great aid here. It enables us to appreciate other times, peoples, and

---

1. Albert Guerard, *France: A Modern History*, p. 15.

cultures; other types of minds, ideals, and governments. It enriches our own civilization by making us more aware that the men who trod this planet before us developed an infinite diversity of ideas, customs, and institutions.

How often one hears it said that the people of a certain nation have no political sense, that they spend all their time bringing down cabinets, quarreling over trifles, and threatening civil war. If we read the history of such a people, however, we are likely to discover that in the past they have been so often conquered by foreign enemies, duped by domestic tyrants, and exploited by both, that they have come to regard government itself as an enemy. We may still think their attitude absurd but at least we now know why it exists and why it has come to be almost instinctive to the people concerned. For an intelligent person who wants to understand any contemporary situation there is no substitute for learning its history.

History for Pleasure and Inspiration — Not the least of reasons for studying history is that it is great literature. Now, to be sure, few people find history immediately entertaining. This is not surprising, though, for it requires concentration, thought, and the acquisition of some fundamental knowledge in order to appreciate anything worthwhile. Once this foundation is acquired history is simultaneously as engrossing, entertaining, and instructive as anything one can read. It is the broadest of all subjects for it deals with every aspect of man's existence. The heights to which man's spirit has ascended, the depths to which it has fallen, the most grandiose conceptions of the human mind, the most magnificent individual and collective feats of courage, the cosmic follies to which mankind has been addicted — all these form the warp and woof of history. It is the tapestry of human existence, and a far richer and more varied one than could be woven by the most imaginative novelist. Think of Washington's ragged, freezing, starving army at Valley Forge; of the German Emperor Henry IV crossing the Alps in the dead of winter (1077) and then standing barefoot in the snow at Canossa for three days, waiting for Pope Gregory VII to grant him an audience; of the explorer Columbus and his men sailing into an unknown ocean in three tiny ships to search for the fabled coast of Asia untold thousands of miles away; of the conquistadores, Pizarro and Cortez, leading pitiful corporals' guards through fire, slaughter, and fabulous adventure into the hearts of rich and mighty empires; of the incredible obstacles encountered and overcome by Sir Ernest Shackleton and his intrepid band of

Antarctic explorers in 1915; of the mad king of Sweden, Charles XII, miraculously escaping harm as twenty-two of twenty-four litter bearers were killed carrying him about in the midst of the battle of Poltava; of the sickening horrors that went on daily in Nazi concentration camps; of the fantastic, monstrous crimes of the devil-worshipping Gilles de Rais, once a Marshal of France and companion of Joan of Arc; of the career of Joan of Arc herself, the inspired peasant girl who restored the elan of the French army in the Hundred Years War and was rewarded with betrayal and a witch's death at the stake; of the sixteenth century Archbishop of Canterbury, Thomas Cranmer, facing death at the stake, thrusting his right hand into the fire in order that the hand which had, in a moment of weakness, signed a recantation of his religious beliefs, might be burned first. These are but a few among thousands of the most marvelous episodes in man's sojourn on earth. Who can read of them without being moved to wonder, admiration, fear, pity, disgust, or tears? These are the deeds of which men have been capable — and of which we too, presumably, are to some degree capable, for how many of us, after all, do as much as we can for either good or ill?

Other branches of learning study a part of man's existence or activities: his mind, his literature, his religious sentiments, or his governmental experiments. History studies everything that man has ever been or tried to be.

CHAPTER II

How To Study History

Study — The first and most fundamental requirement for success in any field, academic or otherwise, is willingness to work. No lazy person ever did well in a history course taught seriously in a reputable college. History is not intrinsically difficult. Unlike astrophysics or the higher reaches of mathematics, which can be comprehended only by superior minds, there is little in history that cannot be understood by a person of normal intelligence. History does, however, require persistent, systematic study. A typical course covers a considerable period of time and deals with a vast array of facts. It usually involves a sizeable quantity of assigned reading. Almost invariably the best history students are those who read assigned materials carefully and do not let themselves "get behind."

Read Extensively — It is highly beneficial to read outside the assignments too. Of all major subjects history is perhaps the most easily self-taught. It is, after all, the story of the past; and one can read this for himself in the same way that he can read about anything else. The lectures of the instructor, classroom discussion, workbook exercises, reports, term papers, and examinations are all important aids to learning but, as a general rule, other things being roughly equal, the person who reads the most history learns the most. A good habit to acquire, where the college library is the open shelf type, is to spend some spare time browsing. Pick up a book at random. Thumb through it. If your eye lights on a passage that looks interesting read until you grow tired of it. If the book proves dull, put it back and try something else. Or, take down a volume of a good encyclopedia and read the articles that strike your fancy. Encyclopedias are mines of information about everything. Of course this sort of thing is no substitute for careful, systematic reading of daily assignments, but it is a valuable auxiliary. What a person is "assigned" he reads to some extent out of a sense of duty, because he knows it is "good for him." What he reads willingly, out of sheer personal interest, he is apt to remember longer. Learning is always up to the individual, fundamentally. The best teacher in the world can coax, threaten — and sometimes inspire — but eighty per cent of learning has always to come from the student's own efforts.

It is easy to coordinate assigned and casual reading. Suppose a day's assignment concerns France at the turn of the fourteenth century. In the reading such names and terms as Philip IV, Nogaret, Flotte, Estates-General, and Templars stand out. After the assignment is finished try reading the articles about these individuals and organizations in the *Encyclopedia Britannica*. One ought not to feel obligated to do this for every assignment, of course, else the extra reading will come to seem like merely more regular work. However, if casual supplemental reading of this sort is done with some consistency for several months the student will find that he has learned a great deal more than if he had read only what was required. In all likelihood, too, the course will have become more enjoyable. It is a truth as old as the world that with interest and learning one and one make three. The more one learns about a subject the more interesting it becomes. The greater one's interest the more eagerly he studies to learn still more.

Here the skeptic may raise the objection that, while he likes to read, he prefers fiction to non-fiction. This condition is only a matter of habit and unwholesome tradition. Many a person gets the idea fixed in his mind when young that reading fiction is fun but reading non-fiction is study or work, and therefore dull. This is not true. To be sure, some of the finest products of the human mind are in the form of fictional literature. Moreover, there are great historical novels that are both entertaining and informative. (Tolstoy's *War and Peace* is a good example.) Nevertheless, a vast amount of fiction is of no consequence whatever. As a generalization, non-fiction is much more apt to be worth reading. Once one forms the habit of reading non-fiction he comes to enjoy it at least as much as even the best fiction and to appreciate that he can learn more from it. It is mostly a matter of training oneself for a time until a good habit is formed.

Take Notes — History deals with a vast array of facts. Because the human memory is a fallible instrument and cannot contain all these the student must somehow condense them to convenient dimensions. The best way is to take notes. It is easy to imagine in September that memory alone will suffice but by the end of the semester or year one will be amazed at how many details, and even matters of major significance, he once "knew" have now completely slipped his mind. No matter how industrious a person might be, how attentive in class, or how interested in the course, his memory is just not efficient enough to store thousands of facts in neat, accurate order and keep them there for months. Some sort of pencil-and-paper system has to make good the deficiency. There is no substitute for a good set of notes when the time comes to review for an important examination.

A side benefit of note-taking is that the mere act of writing something causes a person to remember it better than if he merely reads it or hears it. After class it is a good practice to type the notes taken. Some teachers guarantee at least a "C" to any student who does this faithfully: "guarantee" it in the sense that the practice itself will cause one to learn enough to earn a "C." If one's schedule permits it is a good idea to glance over one's notes for the previous day before going to class. It refreshes one's memory about the context into which the coming day's material will fall.

There are as many note-taking systems as there are students. The best practice is to try several and decide which one seems best for oneself. There are, however, a number of cautions that apply, whatever the system. First of all, take notes selectively and don't take too many. If one takes pages of notes on every assignment it requires so much time that he soon feels the course to be a heavy burden, consuming time that ought to be spent on other subjects. Moreover, a stack of 300 pages of notes at the end of the semester will not prove very useful for review purposes. One might as well read the textbook again. The basic problem, then, is to get a good, usable set of notes without this taking too much time. The first trap to avoid is needless repetition. Either take notes in class and supplement them from the assigned reading or take basic notes from the reading and add to them matters of some importance which come up in class but are not in the reading. Whichever one does ought to depend on the character of the class and the teacher. If the instructor is a systematic lecturer who regularly discusses most of the important matters in the assignment it is probably better to take notes from his lectures and later add to them peripheral matters which he omitted. If the class period is devoted largely to questions-and-answers and discussion it is probably better to take notes on assigned readings and supplement them with points emphasized in class.

Assignments from library books which the student does not own and to which he does not have unlimited, convenient access, should always be summarized in note form. When assignments are from textbooks which the student owns and has in his possession every day he may be well advised not to take notes at all but merely to underline and write in the margins. This is untidy, to be sure, and the resale value of the books may be rendered nil, but it indubitably saves time. If one tries this and finds it satisfactory it will leave him more time for the casual library reading noted above. Remember, the object is to learn, and to do so as efficiently as possible. Study techniques of any sort are of no value in themselves. They should always be measured against the ultimate objective.

Just as there is no "best way" to take notes there is no proper mathematical proportion of notes-to-original-material. In general, if one is assigned ten to twenty-five pages of reading from the library he ought to take a page or two of notes; seldom more than two, and frequently less. Usually it is not a good idea to take notes page-by-page as one goes along since, until the end of the assignment is reached, it is often difficult to tell what is important and what merely explanatory. A better practice is to read the entire assignment, think for a few minutes about its significance, and then try to summarize it in a page or two. After the summary is completed then thumb back through the reading and add to the summary anything of consequence that might have been omitted.

As for the assignments themselves, they should normally be read twice. Probably the best practice is to read the whole assignment rapidly the first time in order to get in mind its main features; and then to read it more slowly and carefully a second time. Some students, however, get good results reading carefully the first time and then re-reading only those portions which are unclear or not completely understood. As with note-taking, try all the alternatives and settle on the one that works best for you.

Use Common Sense — Unquestionably the worst single mistake that many students make when they undertake the study of history is to abandon the common sense bestowed on them at birth. If one reads a book, a newspaper, or a magazine article he does so with the idea of trying to learn what the thing in question is all about. Study history the same way. Try to learn as much as possible about the *facts* of history, the reasons for those facts, the importance of them, and the consequences that have flowed from them. This means, above all, striving to *understand* the past; not merely committing to memory a lot of miscellaneous unconnected information. To spend one's time composing lists of names and dates to be memorized is about as profitable as memorizing the types of birds to be found in the Congo or the names of all the girls in Philadelphia. As soon as the course is over information acquired in this way will soon be forgotten. This is not to say that a knowledge of names and dates is useless. After all, things do not happen "in general"; they happen to specific persons at specific times and places. If one's knowledge of history is not precise and accurate then he does not know history any more than he can be said to "know" any other matter about which all his ideas are haphazard and hazy. The point is that there is a much easier and more logical way to learn with precision than by brute memorization.

Suppose a day's assignment concerns the Carolingian Empire. How pointless to say to oneself, "Now I have to remember what happened in 751, 800, 814, 843, and 888; and I had better make a list of all these names that appear several times — Pepin, Mayors of the Palace, Alcuin, Louis the Pious, Charles the Bald. . . . That's probably what we will be asked on an exam." Surely the common sense procedure is rather to try to become well acquainted with the chief characteristics of the Carolingian Empire, to learn the reasons for its rise and decline, and to understand its importance in the history of Europe as a whole. If a student accomplishes this then he has learned something useful and something that will stick in his mind for years afterward. Furthermore, he will find that in the process of studying for *understanding* he will remember more about the pertinent details (Alcuin, Pepin, 800) than if he had deliberately tried to remember only these isolated facts. This is so because nobody can truly understand anything in general without some accurate knowledge of its details while it is quite possible to memorize details about anything without understanding the larger situation at all.

Consider another example. One may memorize the names and dates of the six members of the Stuart dynasty who ruled England at various times between 1603 and 1714. But what good is such information to anyone unless he is to appear on a quiz program? However, if one knows something about the antecedents of the dynasty as a whole, the personalities and characters of its first four members (James I, Charles I, Charles II, and James II), the religious beliefs and ambitions of these men, the religious ideas of the Puritans, the ambitions of Parliament to secure a larger share in the government of England, the conviction of the Stuarts that Parliament's role should be reduced rather than expanded, and the two civil wars that occurred in seventeenth century England — if one understands these matters then he has learned something important. He now knows how and why the English government assumed much of its modern form; a form widely imitated in the United States and many other parts of the world.

When doing an assignment think about the meaning of the material. Consider how differently things might have turned out had this or that factor been changed or absent. A helpful practice is to make up questions and then try to answer them. How was it possible for the North and the South in the United States to work out compromises about slavery and other sectional differences for forty years and then to prove unable to do this in 1861? Why was the government of Czarist Russia able to suppress an attempted revolution in the midst of a losing war in 1905 but unable to suppress another such revolution in the midst of the First World War in 1917? What conditions had changed? What personal factors were different? What was the crucial consideration? Why was Napoleon Bonaparte able to score an unbroken succession of victories over a variety of opponents for fifteen years and then, within three years, 1812-1815, suffer crushing defeats at the hands of these same opponents in Russia, at Leipzig, and at Waterloo? Why were primitive parliaments first organized in widely scattered parts of Europe at about the same time, the thirteenth and early fourteenth centuries, when no part of Europe had known anything resembling representative government for over a thousand years? Population increases, the rise of the middle class, the ambitions of a number of kings, and the need of governments for more money, all had something to do with it. But which of these (and other) factors was most important?

If one is to answer questions of this sort he must do more than learn factual information. He must think about what he reads; think of what he has learned about similar situations encountered earlier in the course; think about what he, personally, has observed of the ways of men in his own lifetime. Lastly, he has to try to put all this together and make a judgment about it. This is not easy. Often the judgment will be wrong. Often it will be impossible for anyone to say beyond question that the judgment is or is not correct. But one thing is certain: the student who approaches history in this way will learn and understand far more than the one who merely memorizes in order to pass tomorrow's quiz.

Become Historically Minded — History is not a series of unconnected episodes, all about equally important or equally useless, each embellished with a chapter title, and all then assembled in a book. It is a seamless garment, each part of which is related to all the others. It should be studied as such: studied with the object of understanding how civilizations change and why; how societies differ in many ways yet usually have to face the same kinds of problems; how innumerable ideas, events, and institutions from the past have made our present world what it is.

Any history course is centered around certain themes or developments. The student's understanding will be facilitated if he thinks of a particular assignment as it fits into some over-all pattern. Consider a couple of typical courses of the "survey" type, one in European history and one in American history. Most European "survey" courses begin the first semester with ancient Greece and end somewhere around 1650-1715. One main theme in such a course is the way several ancient cultures were blended to form what eventually became European civilization. Greek achievement in the arts and sciences, Roman law and government, Christian theological and ethical concepts, and the customs of the Germanic peoples, were all fused into a composite whole in the first six or seven centuries of the Christian era.

Another useful way of regarding the first semester of European history is to think of it as church history. The Christian Church was founded in a hostile society. Little by little its doctrinal and organizational structure developed. It made converts, was beset by heresy, vexed by internal corruption, and troubled by quarrels with civil rulers. Schisms between its eastern and western members were frequent. The last such schism, in the eleventh century, divided Christendom into Greek Orthodox and Roman Catholic halves. In the fifteenth century it was threatened with a similar split in the West, and in the sixteenth century it was shattered into fragments by the Protestant Reformation. In the last instance radically different conceptions of Christianity were developed. Any one day's assignment will become more meaningful if viewed in its relationship to this general process.

From another point of view, much of the first semester of European history can be regarded as the story of the growth of central governments. Following the breakup of the Carolingian Empire in the ninth century centralized government virtually ceased to exist in Europe. Then for the next seven hundred years kings little by little added to their powers and whittled away at those of their rivals. They posed as God's special agents for ruling men. They played off one feudal noble against another. As trade grew and the middle class became more numerous kings gradually came to employ middle class people in their administrations. These men of common birth had no personal or family power. Hence they were easier to control, and therefore more loyal to their employers, than feudal aristocrats. In a variety of ways kings gradually extended their control over the church in their dominions. As they acquired more money they came to depend less and less on feudal knights to do their fighting. Instead they hired professional soldiers who could on occasion be used *against* the knights. After the invention of the crossbow, the longbow and, especially, gunpowder, a king's professional troops could easily defeat feudal knights who scorned to use these unchivalrous, but deadly, new weapons. With the coming of the Protestant Reformation in the sixteenth century the religious unity of Christendom was split. Instead of one universal church there were now a great number of churches. In both Catholic and Protestant countries, consequently, kings were able to dominate churches to a greater degree than formerly. Altogether, by 1650 European kings had far more real power in their realms and far more influence over the lives of their subjects than had their royal ancestors six or seven hundred years earlier. As one progresses through the first semester of European history he should keep this general development in mind. If the day's assignment deals with the growth of trade in the thirteenth century, the Hundred Years War, or the Great Western Schism, he should ask himself, "Does this event tend to increase the power of kings and their central administrations, does it tend to decrease it, or does it have no bearing on that question? How? Why? In what ways? Was this immediately evident at the time or did it become clear only much later?

Suppose the course concerns the history of the United States from the Civil War to the present. What are some of the main themes that run through most of the past century in American life? One, obviously, is the growth of what is sometimes called the Welfare State. With only occasional interruptions or temporary reversals, the U.S. Government has tended with every passing generation to make more laws about more things, to regulate more closely the activities of private individuals, to spend more money in more ways, and to feel a greater responsibility for the economic welfare of all its citizens.

In foreign affairs perhaps the broadest general trend has been the increasing interest taken by our country in the rest of the world. In the last half of the nineteenth century this interest was centered primarily in Latin America. Around 1900 it was clearly extending to the Far East. By 1917 we had intervened in a major European war. In World War II we fought two major wars in widely separated parts of the world — at the same time. Since 1945 we have become closely concerned with events in every part of the globe.

Another significant development in the past century has been that the United States has changed from a largely agricultural nation to the world's foremost industrial power. A metamorphosis of this sort necessarily involves basic alterations in the manner of life of much of the population. It requires packing millions of people into cities. Immediately, depressions and subsequent unemployment present incomparably more serious problems than they ever had when most people were small farmers who could, in the last analysis, grow enough food to live no matter what economic conditions might be in general. Thus industrialization soon meant the organization of labor unions, strife between these bodies and the owners of industry, and the growth of socialism and other doctrines either critical of industrialism itself or desirous of managing the system in some different way than by private ownership. When the student reads of Manifest Destiny, the Pullman Strike, the McKinley Tariff, the Social Security system, or the Marshall Plan, he ought at once to ask himself what is its connection with these major tendencies in American history.

Nothing better facilitates the process of becoming historically minded than to put one's mind back into the past and look from that time forward. This requires some imagination and practice, but it improves one's understanding of the past immeasurably. The deeds of men long since dead often seems stupid and futile. This is not surprising for who is not wiser afterward than he was at the time he had to make some decision? But one must always think of the circumstances in which men act. Who can foresee the future or calculate all the consequences of his actions? Every person alive now has to think and plan and act on the basis of what he knows *now* and the way things apear to him *now;* not on the basis of what *will be known* 500 years from now. So it has always been. To merely praise or denounce the beliefs and deeds of past societies is fruitless. If one wants to understand what long dead individuals thought and did, and why, he has to try to put himself in their shoes and to see their problems *as they saw them.*

Suppose a day's assignment deals with the feudal system. This is a subject that frequently seems fantastic and unreal to twentieth century students. Why, the student thinks, should 90% of the population have lived in rude huts and spent much of their time working for a few lords and knights who lived in castles and spent their lives hunting, fighting, romancing, and attending tournaments? And who ever thought of all those silly feudal institutions: fiefs, homage, investiture, vassals, and the rest? What an absurd way to organize society! Instead of reading about feudalism with these thoughts in mind the student should try to imagine himself living in the tenth century. What was life like then? To begin with, the general condition of most men was one of desperate poverty. Agricultural implements were crude, farm animals small and poor, modern scientific agriculture unknown, and crop yields pitifully meagre. Famine was commonplace. There were no roads worthy of the name. Save for the nobility, who owned horses, travel was generally confined to the distances that a man could walk. Many a peasant never in his life ventured ten miles from the place of his birth. Schools were unknown save in an occasional monastery or royal court. Since coined money had largely disappeared in western Europe kings had little cash with which to maintain either bureaucracies to govern their realms or standing armies to defend them. The chief reward they could give to their retainers for military or other services was land. Each gift of land weakened the king who gave and strengthened the noble who received. In these conditions the only protection the peasant had against Viking invaders from the north, Moslem invaders from the south, or bands of professional robbers from his own society, was that afforded him by the castle and the armed knights of the great lord in his immediate locality. The lord and knights did not extend this protection for nothing. They demanded in return work on their lands, payment in money, payment in services, and payment in agricultural produce. The price was high but the peasant had no alternative.

In these circumstances what must lord and peasant have thought of each other? What changes had to take place in the world before a society of this type could become the society we know now? It is thoughts of this sort that ought to be going through the mind of the student as he reads about feudalism. If he does so ponder the matter he will appreciate much better the reasons for fiefs, homage, vassals, and all the rest, than if he merely sinks himself into a soft chair, switches on the desk lamp, and reads unthinkingly about these feudal institutions.

Nothing is commoner in history than issuing indiscriminate praise or sweeping condemnations of long dead individuals — without giving a thought to the problems they had to face or the way those problems looked to men at the time. A good case in point is that of the Renaissance Pope Clement VII, 1523-1534. History has not been kind to Pope Clement. He is usually depicted as a shifty, indecisive fellow; a man insufficiently aware of the seriousness and implications of the Protestant Revolt; a bungler who handled the Henry VIII-Catherine of Aragon annulment case so badly that one of the most powerful kings in Europe deserted Catholicism and took his country into the Protestant camp. Before one passes off Clement VII as a mere blunderer, however, he ought to consider the whole European religious and diplomatic situation as it appeared to that Pontiff in the years 1527-1531.

To begin with, King Henry VIII of England, for a variety of motives, some personal and some political, wished to have his marriage to his queen, Catherine of Aragon, annulled so that he might marry Anne Boleyn. Many years before Henry had had to apply to Rome for a Papal dispensation to marry Catherine at all. This was needed since she had previously been married to Henry's elder brother, now dead. (A passage in the Bible forbade marriage to a brother's widow.) The dispensation had been granted by Pope Julius II, the marriage had taken place, and Henry and Catherine had lived as man and wife for eighteen years. But the king eventually tired of Catherine and wanted to wed Anne. Hence he began to search for pretexts to dissolve the marriage. He first insisted that there were technical flaws in the original dispensation. Clement VII's canon lawyers could not find any. Then the king argued that Pope Julius had had no right to grant the dispensation in the first place because the Bible expressly forbade a man to marry his brother's widow. Papal theologians considered this point and decided that Henry's understanding of the Bible was faulty. This put the Pope in a dilemma. Sweden had already renounced its religious allegiance to Rome. The Lutheran movement was gaining adherents rapidly in Germany. King Francis I of France was an ambitious, unscrupulous monarch who periodically showed favor to Protestants in order to extract concessions from the Papacy. At times he even intimated that he might turn Protestant himself. If he should do so he would take with him millions of his subjects in one of Europe's strongest and most populous nations. The Holy Roman Emperor was the Hapsburg, Charles V. He and Francis I were by far the most powerful rulers in Europe. They spent much of their time making war against each other. The Pope dared not alienate Francis lest the King of France turn Protestant, whereby France would be lost to Catholicism. Yet if he showed favor to Francis this would be resented by Charles V, and the Pope did not dare to antagonize him either. He did not trust Charles because the Papacy had struggled for centuries to secure independence from just such overmighty Holy Roman Emperors as Charles V. Finally, Clement feared for the safety of his own kingdom, the Papal States, because Italy had been the battleground of French and Hapsburg armies for the preceding generation, and Papal military and political strength was far too feeble to cope with either Francis or Charles.

In these circumstances Henry VIII pressed for his annulment. What was Pope Clement VII to do? He already had troubles of the utmost seriousness on every side. The last thing he would want to do would be to alienate still another powerful king, a man who had heretofore been the most faithful crowned friend of the Papacy in Europe. Nothing would have pleased Clement more than to have granted the King of England's request. Yet, as Papal experts in those matters saw it, Henry had no case in either law or theology. Moreover, Catherine, Henry's wife, opposed the annulment. And Catherine was the aunt of the distressingly mighty Charles V!

In 1527 one of Charles V's armies mutinied near Rome and took the Pope prisoner. Now the Pontiff's position seemed truly hopeless. He could not give a decision in favor of Henry, both because he was convinced that Henry had no case and because he was the prisoner of Catherine's nephew, the powerful Emperor. He feared to decide definitely against Henry for this might mean the loss of England's religious allegiance to Rome. So Clement resolutely did nothing at all. He held inquiries, wrote letters, appointed commissions, suggested compromises and reconciliations: in short, he tried everything he could think of to stall for time and therefore avoid having to make a decision at all. He hoped that something would change: Henry would die, Catherine would die, Anne Boleyn would die, Henry would see the error of his theological opinions and withdraw his request, Henry would lose interest in Anne, Henry and Catherine would become reconciled — that something, anything, would happen to solve the problem without the necessity of making an official Papal pronouncement.

Now this was not a very heroic attitude, to be sure, but it was not an unreasonable one for, after all, time *does* solve many problems. Innumerable tangles, from which there seemed no way out at the time, have unravelled themselves with the death of an interested party or two, a change of mind after reflection, or a change of circumstances. But, Clement had no luck. None of these things transpired. Instead Henry gradually lost patience with Papal delays, withdrew England's religious allegiance to Rome, got his annulment from one of his own clerical appointees in England, and married Anne. At the end of it all the Pope appeared to have played a sorry role. He had procrastinated in the most undignified manner, and all to no avail.

It is reasonably clear now, more than 400 years after these events, that the Pope would have been wiser to have taken a strong stand, at the outset, for what he believed right; to have flatly denied Henry's request without regard for the consequences. He might have lost England, to be sure (but, then, he lost it anyway), but his action would have heartened many who had become disillusioned with Rome in recent years and he would have gone down in history as a brave man who stood by principle. But all this is being wise after the event. What the student should ask himself is, "What would I have done had I been Pope Clement VII? How would I have faced that situation? What decision would I have made, not knowing what the future would bring? Would I have stood out at once for what I thought to be the right of the matter or would I, too, have played for time and hoped for some luck?" If one thinks of the whole question in this fashion he may still be convinced that Clement VII lacked both judgment and heroism, or he may not, but at least he will understand that not all problems are simple, not all decisions are easy, not all solutions are obvious.

Similar thoughts are induced by a consideration of the career of Bismarck. Prince Otto von Bismarck was Chancellor of Prussia, 1862-1871, and Chancellor of the German Empire, 1871-1890. By general consent, he was the cleverest and most influential European statesman of his age. During his Chancellorship Germany grew rapidly in wealth and industrial strength, acquired overseas colonies, developed a large, efficient army that made her the world's mightiest land power, and formed a complex system of alliances by which she was bound to or had amicable understandings with all Europe's major powers save only her old enemy, France. And France had no allies at all! On the military and diplomatic side much of this was the personal achievement of Bismarck, the virtual ruler of the German Empire until his retirement in 1890.

Yet there are many twentieth century historians who hold that Bismarck was a calamity for Germany. Their argument runs roughly as follows: 1) The military tradition was already disagreeably strong in Germany. Bismarck made it worse in at least two different ways. He unified the scattered German states in three short, aggressive wars. In domestic German politics he habitually bullied parliaments and had recourse to threats of force in order to gain his way. 2) The alliance system which Bismarck devised was inhumanly complicated and full of internal contradictions. It could be managed only by a trickster of genius like Bismarck himself. After he retired control of German policy fell into the hands of second and third rate men. Soon the alliance system assumed a new form. Countries once tied to Germany became hostile, and in a generation most of Europe was fighting Germany in the First World War. 3) The constitution which Bismarck gave to Germany in 1871 was a sham. The relationship between the Emperor and the Chancellor was left undefined because Bismarck knew he could always dominate the Emperor William I on a man-to-man basis. The Reichstag or German parliament was just a debating society because Bismarck disliked the whole business of voting, speech-making, and heeding elected assemblies. Finally, the constitution left the position of the army ambiguous. Instead of taking an oath to the nation or to its constitution German officers took an oath to the Emperor as a person. Instead of the army being subject to the Reichstag, as would have been the case in countries like the United States or England where parliamentary government was genuine, the German army was made responsible only to the Crown.

Thus, say Bismarck's critics, the Iron Chancellor intensified militarism in Germany; he established a tradition of deceit and trickery, and showed that it could be made to yield great gains; and he brought parliamentary government into disrepute in a country where too many people were already willing to follow any leader who was "successful." Finally, his peculiar constitution of 1871, so full of ambiguities, was tailored only for himself. Once he had passed from the scene Germany was left without a stable government. Logically, Bismarck's legacy was Hitler's movement and two world wars.

This analysis raises interesting questions. Should Bismarck really be blamed for failing to foresee what kind of harvest would result from the seeds he had sown? To what extent can any man foresee the future and plan for it? Even supposing that one can foresee to some degree what his principles portend, is it really possible for him to make arrangements in his lifetime that will enable him to determine his country's policies for any appreciable period after his death? What answer could one give to Bismarck if he should now rise from the grave and say in his own defense, "When I was Chancellor, when the governing of Germany was in my hands, Germany was the greatest nation in Europe, Europe was at peace, and our national enemy (France) was isolated and powerless to attack us. Why blame me for what William II and Hitler did years after my death? Are the deeds of all German bunglers from 1890 to the end of time *my* responsibility? I was not Master of the Universe for All the Ages. I was only Chancellor of Prussia and Germany, 1862-1890. On *that* I should be judged."

How to Become Historically Minded — A sense of history can be developed in a number of specific, tangible ways. One of the best is to make personal contacts with the past. Visit historical museums. Think of the origins and meaning of national holidays, religious holidays, religious ceremonies, and local pageants and festivals. Ponder the origins of various foods, implements, styles of clothing, ideas — and even words. Many words in English usage are of French, Celtic, Arabic, African, or other origin. One acquires a sense of history in finding out when and in what circumstances they became part of the English language. For example, various African words might have come into English usage from contacts with West African slave traders.

When travelling do not merely look but think of the implications of what you see. In most parts of the world one can readily see innumerable evidences of the past. A visit to the walled city of Carcassone in southern France or the town of Rothenberg in Germany immediately carries one back into the atmosphere of the Middle Ages. The restoration of Williamsburg, Virginia, to its condition in colonial times similarly transports the visitor back into America's past. Sometimes the contrasts between present and past are immediate and vivid within a very limited area. In many European cities, for example, one may stroll about inside a cathedral or town hall centuries old and then step outside into a traffic jam reminiscent of today's New York or Chicago. One may drive through the countryside and see one French or Italian farm family cultivating their acres with horses, a second employing the most up-to-date farm machinery, and a third using oxen. Across the road may be a modern oil refinery. Everywhere in our daily lives we make innumerable contacts with the past if we but observe them and give them a passing thought.

Another excellent way to develop an interest, understanding, and appreciation of history is to read serious newspapers and magazines. An appallingly large number of young people seem to think that there is no connection between what they study in school and what goes on in the world about them. How can one possibly claim to be a "student," in pursuit of learning, when he does not read newspapers, listen to news broadcasts, or have any but the vaguest notion about what is taking place either in his own country or elsewhere in the world? Newspapers and newsmagazines are contemporary history. Just as knowledge of the past improves one's judgment about the present, so a knowledge of what goes on in the world now will make a history course more interesting and meaningful. Every student should listen to news broadcasts daily and spend at least two hours a week reading some reputable newspaper or newsmagazine as carefully and thoughtfully as he would prepare a class assignment. Whenever some country, issue, or situation is persistently in the news one should try to read a book or serious article on its background or on some similar past situation.

Examinations — About no subject is absurdity and superstition so rampant as examinations. Nine times out of ten the student who is intelligent, has done well in class on a day-to-day basis, and has allowed himself time to prepare for an important examination, will do well on it, whether the test be the essay type, true-and-false, completion, identification, or multiple choice. Similarly the person who is not intelligent, has not studied, or doesn't allow himself time to prepare, will almost certainly do badly. Nearly anyone, however, whatever his abilities and industry, can usually do somewhat better if he heeds a few common sense principles.

1) *How to Study* — When preparing for a major history examination the first consideration is to allow sufficient time to review and think about the course thus far. Two or three hours a day for perhaps three days before a mid-term examination, and the same amount of time for four or five days before a final examination, ought to be a minimum. This much careful, systematic study will fix in mind many details and illustrations with which examination essays can be embellished and, lacking which, those essays will seem

thin to the corrector. One should review in the same way that he has studied for the course. Read over several times the notes taken in class or on outside readings. Go through the textbook, reading where it is underlined or where writing appears in the margins. If you are sure you know a given section quite well skim over it rapidly. If you feel confused or frankly ignorant about a section, then read it carefully and resume skimming thereafter. In all cases think of the meaning of the course thus far, the chief trends that have emerged, the main problems encountered, the way one condition has gradually become another, and why.

Sometimes it is useful for several students to study together and to discuss different features of the course. A word of caution is in order here, however. Stick to business and do not let the discussion degenerate into a mere "bull session." Also, make sure that there is at least one person present who does well in·the course. A good or excellent student can sometimes improve his own performance by helping others since he must necessarily clarify his own thinking about a subject in order to explain it to someone else. However, several students who have difficulty with a subject and who study together are more apt to compound the confusion than to learn much from each other.

2) *Essay Questions* — Short answer questions of whatever type are either right or wrong and there is little advice one can give the student about them save that he had better know the material. Essay questions, however, present a few problems of tactics and techniques. First and foremost, read the directions. If the instruction is to answer three out of five questions then do *three* of them. Do not do four or five in hope of getting extra credit, or in the hope that the *best* three will be counted. Most likely the grader will read only the first three anyway. Moreover, the time allotted will be what is regarded as sufficient to do three essays *well*. If the time is spent doing four or five all will have to be skimped. Likewise, divide the time about equally among the essays. If forty-five minutes is allowed to do three essays spend about fifteen minutes on each; not twenty minutes apiece on two of them and five minutes on the last one. Of course, if you know two of them well and the third hardly at all it is better to do two very thoroughly and to try at least to get good grades on them than to waste ten minutes puzzling about something you don't know anyway. Remember, though, one of the first thoughts that is apt to pass through the corrector's mind is this: "The student had fifteen minutes to

answer this question. How much could a person reasonably be expected to write in that time if he knew this matter well? Maybe a page, or a page and a half, or two, depending in part on how large his handwriting happens to be." If the corrector then encounters a four-sentence answer he is not likely to be impressed, even though the four sentences may be correct as far as they go.

Before starting to write anything read the question carefully and think about it for a minute or two. Be sure that you understand it, and that you answer the question asked — not some other one. Any teacher will testify that he has read dozens of respectable essays relating vaguely to the question asked but not really answering it. If you know little about a particular subject it is, of course, better to write around it than to write nothing at all, for you may thus get *some* credit. But only *some* credit will seldom be enough to enable one to pass an examination — or a course.

After thinking about the question for a moment and making sure you understand it, formulate the answer in your mind. Make certain that you get the main points in that answer down on paper. Either write them down at once and then use the rest of the essay to explain them, or else make sure that you bring each one into the ·essay in its proper place. The essay itself should be a blend of generalizations and specific factual detail: not one or the other, but both. A student who has a good mind but studies little will often remember the main ideas in a history course but will seldom recall much in the way of illustrative details. His essays, consequently, usually consist mostly of generalities, which may well fit the situation in question — but fit other historical problems and periods almost equally well.

Another student who has marginal natural ability but who works hard may have considerable difficulty understanding ideas and general concepts but be able to memorize much specific information. His essays are apt to be masses of factual detail, often largely or entirely correct, but leading nowhere in particular and showing no comprehension of the relevance of these happenings to anything else. A good essay, much easier to describe than to produce, but the ideal to strive for nonetheless, is a combination of these two.

Suppose, for example, that one is to write an essay on this question: "Discuss the foreign and domestic policies of Richelieu." A good way to begin would be to devote two or three sentences to a description of the situation facing Richelieu when he came to power in 1624. Then think of the main ideas. Richelieu's chief domestic ambition was to increase the power of the king over all groups and classes in France. Start a paragraph with that. Then illustrate the point by discussing Richelieu's dealings with the nobles and the Huguenots, his military reforms, and his changes in the French administration. Indicate, as time permits, the opposition aroused by these policies and how the opponents were dealt with. Then begin the second part of the essay with the main generalization about Richelieu's foreign policy: he wanted to increase the power of France in relation to that of other European states. Illustrate this by references to his activities in the Thirty Years War and his dealings with England and Spain. Note in passing that some of the things he did or attempted had repercussions in both domestic and foreign affairs; and that the strengthening of the Crown inside France was a necessary prelude to the effort to make the nation mighty abroad. Conclude with a couple of sentences about Richelieu's relative success or failure and the general significance of his achievements: e.g., did they permanently affect the character of the French Government? Did they have any lasting effects on the fortunes of the Huguenots or the French nobility?

Last and by no means least, write respectable English — and in complete sentences. It is shameful that such an admonition should need to be addressed to students, but anyone who has read many of their papers knows that it must be. To write in a correct, grammatical, civilized manner ought to be a matter of pride. One who has spent ten or twelve consecutive years in school should be ashamed to write in the jargon of pocket-book private detectives or Western Union telegrams. What is the purpose of studying one's native language, of taking English Composition courses, if one does not attempt to use what he has learned in all his writing?

Even putting ideals aside and descending to the lowest "practical" level, a well-written essay will ordinarily get a better grade than one with the same factual content but filled with abbreviations, misspelled words, grammatical atrocities, advertising mumbo-jumbo, and slang. First impressions count for a lot, and no less with teachers than with others. If a corrector sees a slovenly paper he usually concludes one of two things about its author: 1) He is unintelligent. (He cannot possibly be uneducated, for he has been in school since he was six years old.), or 2) He is lazy and indifferent. Neither conclusion is apt to do the student much good when a mark is put on the paper. Conversely, a corrector will have a good opinion of a student who writes correctly and expresses himself clearly, even though there may be factual errors in his essay. Naturally, the first consideration in marking history papers must be the factual accuracy of the answers, but any doubts or judgments are normally resolved in favor of the person who attempts to write respectably and against the one who does not. All we mortals are ignorant enough. A prudent person will try to avoid appearing more ignorant than he really is.

To sum up: study history by putting your mind back into the period under consideration; study to understand, not memorize; do assignments promptly; take notes; read as much history of all kinds as time permits; pay attention to current events; and prepare carefully for examinations. If one follows these precepts, and is gifted with normal common sense, history will cause him no worries.

CHAPTER III

THINGS ALWAYS CHANGE: BUT ALWAYS REMAIN THE SAME

No Sharp Breaks In History — If one thumbs through his European history textbook he sees it nicely divided into chapters with such titles as: The Decline of the Roman Empire, The Barbarian Invasions, The Byzantine Empire, The Rise of Islam, The Carolingian Interlude, The Rise of National Monarchies, The Decline of the Medieval Church, The Renaissance, The Reformation, and so on. As he reads he encounters such phrases as The Dark Ages, The Age of Faith, The Age of the Enlightenment; The Religious Revolution, The Industrial Revolution, The Scientific Revolution, The French Revolution, and the Russian Revolution; The Century of Skepticism, The Century of Liberalism, and The Century of Totalitarianism. Undoubtedly, he often gets the impression that the course of history is a series of abrupt, radical shifts; that the "Middle Ages" suddenly became a markedly different age called the "Renaissance"; that such a cataclysm as the French Revolution changed Europe out of all recognition; that nearly all Europeans were loyal to monarchy in the eighteenth century, devotees of liberalism in the nineteenth century, and followers of totalitarianism in the twentieth.

The truth is far different. There are no sharp breaks in history. More things always remain the same than ever change. Human nature is much the same at all times. The interests of most people at most times revolve around their families, the way they gain their livelihood, and the problems and activities of their immediate neighborhood. Throughout recorded history tribes and nations have been consistently hostile to other such groups and have tried to conquer them. Men everywhere have regularly, though not always with the same sense of urgency, sought to find better and easier ways of doing their daily tasks. Men have always sought to add to their knowledge. The vast majority of people are always natural conservatives, in the sense that they prefer the known and familiar to the unknown. Men tend to have strong, constant loyalties that are broken down or altered only gradually and with great difficulty: loyalties to religion, to country, to particular forms of government, to social ideas, or to feudal superiors. If some drastic

31

change is proposed, usually more people will have something to lose by it than will have something to gain. This is especially true of the influential people, those who will be in the best position to resist change effectively.

Extent of Change Easily Overrated — Even when seemingly drastic changes do take place the extent of the change is often illusory. Most of the time there is some sort of compromise with things-as-they-were. Much of the old regime is quietly retained but some innovations in both substance and exterior appearance are introduced. If one reflects a bit he will realize that this is inevitable. No government can ever entirely control the minds and activities of all its subjects. No human agency can as yet control man's physical environment. In any given country some problems are constant because it lies in a desert, in the tropics, in the mountains, in the far north, is subject to recurrent floods or earthquakes, or has a strong, aggressive people as an immediate neighbor. The basic mode of life of the country in question will be strongly influenced by these considerations no matter what sort of government or economic system it has.

There is much continuity in human history, too, because of the very nature and structure of government. Any regime has to maintain internal order, to keep up an army to defend its subjects, to translate its principles into laws, to develop an administration to run the country on a day-to-day basis, and to collect from its people the taxes necessary to support these activities. All governments, whether the mildest democracies or the most pitiless despotisms, have to do these things in *some* manner.

A common type in history is the revolutionary idealist, the hot-eyed zealot, the "man of principle" who is going to sweep out some rotten, discredited system and replace it with something totally different and radiantly pure. Sometimes this "man of principle" is able to gain office or power. One of the first things he is apt to discover is that the whole condition he has been denouncing is a lot more complex than he had supposed and that it is much harder to take "decisive action" in practice than it was to talk about it. He discovers that many things cannot be changed at all without alienating whole groups of people without whose support, or at least neutrality, he can do little save continue to make speeches. He finds that he has to rule the country through the existing civil service (since he cannot train his own overnight), and that most of its members have no particular sympathy for his views. Before long our "man of principle" finds himself making compromises of the very sort that he had previously denounced when they were made by other governments. He is able to change the direction of affairs to some degree but in most respects public matters proceed much as before.

But Nothing Remains Stationary — Yet change is a constant factor in human history too. No situation ever remains entirely static. As long as men have minds, imaginations, ambitions, ideals; as long as they love and hate and fear and yearn; as long, in fact, as they remain men; some of them will want to remedy this or that ill, try some new idea or system, seek power for themselves or their friends or their class, or simply strike out in hatred or frustration at what they despise. If things never move rapidly enough for the visionary, neither do they remain sufficiently stable to suit the conservative.

In view of the foregoing considerations textbook divisions and chapter titles may seem largely formal, mechanical, and unreal. This is only partly true. A book has to be divided in *some* fashion and titles given to the various parts, otherwise one would have to conclude that things are so much the same at all times that no divisions are possible. This is plainly ludicrous. Moreover, if all times were alike there would be no point in studying the history of any period but one's own. Even the most conventional textbook divisions mirror reality to a considerable degree.

A good case in point concerns the Renaissance and its real or alleged difference from the Middle Ages. Many historians have seen the Renaissance as one of the great turning points in history, one of man's finest ages. Here, they say, after 1000 years of dreary stagnation and subjugation to religious authority men began to throw off the shackles of the Middle Ages, to take a lively interest in the things of this world, to think for themselves, to take pride in their individual accomplishments; in a word, they ceased to be medieval and became modern. This view has been amusingly caricatured by Andre Maurois, who has a knight addressing his followers thus: "In truth, then, we men of the Middle Ages must not forget that tomorrow we set off for the Hundred Years War."[1] Other scholars argue that the Renaissance was preceded by move-

---

1. Quoted by Douglas Bush, "The Renaissance and English Humanism: Modern Theories of the Renaissance," in Karl H. Dannenfeldt, *The Renaissance: Medieval or Modern?, Heath Problems in European Civilization,* p. 87.

ments so similar to it, and that it came about so gradually, that the whole concept of "Renaissance" has little validity. A few would abolish the word entirely, as introducing unnecessary confusion into the history of an age already sufficiently complex. There is so little agreement among historians in this field that five centuries after the "Renaissance" it is difficult to find two textbooks that ascribe the same dates to this phantom era.

What is the student to do in this impasse? He might begin by putting his mind back into the fourteenth century and asking himself, "Would I have been as aware of the changes taking place as Maurois' knight?" Hardly. Then he might ask himself, "What would I be doing if I were alive in the fourteenth century?" Here the chances are about ten to one that he would be an illiterate peasant in some rural village tending his animals, sowing and harvesting his crops, paying his tithes to the church and his taxes to the seigneur, and hoping that there would not be a famine or a military campaign in his locality this year. He would be living in a fashion very similar to that of his ancestors for twenty or thirty generations. What could mean less to him than this "Renaissance"? Life for peasants, the overwhelming numerical majority of the population, went on much the same in the Renaissance as it always had.

Yet even if we admit that the Renaissance was confined almost entirely to a small number of political figures, scholars, artists, and business people, these are indubitably the persons who lead in this world. Their deeds and opinions, consequently, are important. And in the period, 1350-1550, the outlook and interests of these people changed in many easily perceptible ways. Respect for the civilizations of pagan antiquity grew much more marked, interest in this world and the careers that could be made in it increased, secular motifs became commoner in the fine arts, religious zeal on the highest levels in the church flagged noticeably, geographical exploration was undertaken on an unprecedented scale, and the beginnings of serious, critical historical scholarship appeared. Thus even though the student should never allow himself to forget that the bulk of Europe's people lived and died untouched by these changes, still the innovations were there, and they were sufficiently important and sufficiently different from medieval norms to justify giving a special name, "Renaissance," to these two centuries.

Awareness of Change — Sometimes people are aware that they live in an era of marked, rapid change and sometimes they are not. The ancient writers Salvian and St. Jerome were so shaken by the ravages of the Visigoths and the sacking of Rome by Alaric in 410 A.D. that it seemed to them as if the very world were ending. All that civilized men had always counted on and taken for granted seemed to be crashing to ruins. Another contemporary, however, was much less pessimistic. St. Augustine noted that Rome had recovered from calamities in the past and would doubtless do so this time too.[1] Augustine's reaction was evidently more typical of the populace in general for elsewhere in his writings he complained that Roman citizens paid little attention to the Visigothic marauders, but spent their time instead struggling for seats in the theaters.[2]

A man born in 400 A.D. and living to extreme old age would not have thought that the sun shone any less brightly in the "Dark Ages" of 475, 480, and 490 than it had in the "Roman Empire" era of his childhood. If he knew anything of the past history of Rome or remembered the talk of oldsters when he was a child he would probably have considered that the events of his own lifetime differed only in degree and detail from what had been going on for at least 200 years before. "Barbarians" were invaders now, but then "barbarians" had been inside the Empire in some capacity or other for generations and they had been on its borders for centuries. Roman local government had largely broken down long before the birth of our old Roman, and the civil wars and power struggles of the third and fourth centuries had produced bloodshed and unrest only slightly less persistent and calamitous than in his own time. Thus even if modern learned opinion is virtually unanimous in regarding the collapse of the Roman Empire as one of history's great turning points it is doubtful if many contemporaries were aware that they were living in such a momentous age.

Modern people tend to be more aware of change than the ancients because the tempo of the modern world is far more rapid than at any time in the past and is constantly accelerating. The main reasons for this are: 1) literacy is now virtually universal in the western world, thereby making it possible to circulate new ideas much more widely and rapidly than ever before, and 2) the scientific and industrial advances of the past century have given man an unprecedented power to influence his environment. Consider how much the day-to-day lives and thoughts of scores of millions of ordinary people would be changed if there were no auto-

---

1. St. Augustine, *City of God*, iv, 7.
2. *Ibid.*, i, 33.

mobiles, airplanes, refrigerators, frozen foods, air conditioners, radios, television sets, or mass destruction weapons. Yet none of these things existed seventy years ago. It is little wonder that unthinking people so often feel that things change so swiftly now that there is nothing to be gained by studying the past.

Roots in the Past — Only a little reflection is needed, however, to remind an American that our ties with the distant past are still many and strong. Our governmental institutions and beliefs are derived directly from a series of events, documents, and conceptions nearly 200 years old. More remotely, they are derived from the English constitutional tradition which is at least 700 years old. We are still professedly a Christian nation and thereby formally committed to a set of beliefs and a code of private and public conduct 2000 years old. In literature, the fine arts, and intellectual pursuits generally, we continue to study and admire, if not always to emulate, the works of Kant, Descartes, St. Thomas Aquinas, Goethe, Shakespeare, Michelangelo, Da Vinci, Cicero, Aristotle, Socrates, Plato, and a host of others — a galaxy of luminaries extending backward in time at least to the ancient Greeks.

Modern Communist Russia furnishes many examples of the complex interweaving of change and continuity in human affairs. Post-1917 Russia differs sharply from old Russia in many ways. The whole society is now officially dedicated to Marxism and everything its rulers choose to do is justified by some reference to Marxist principles. Soviet Russia employs government propaganda, concentration camps, police brutality, and state direction of every economic and social activity on a scale without parallel in recorded history. It is officially committed to the eventual abolition of private ownership. By means of communist parties in other countries it maintains throughout the world a vast army of loyal agents vigilant to promote Russian interests at the expense of their own countries and working ceaselessly to communize the entire world. Under communism Russia has become a literate nation and the world's second ranking industrial power. All this seems new. Much of it genuinely is new.

The more one learns of Russian history, however, the more evidences of her past he can see in contemporary Russia. For generations the Czars sought to expand to the east in Siberia and towards Manchuria, Afghanistan, and Persia (now Iran). In the west they sought to expand at the expense of the Swedes and Turks, to control Poland, to gain a "window to the west" on the Baltic, and to secure Constantinople or an outlet on the Adriatic Sea. Communist Russian designs are very similar. Not only Poland but the rest of eastern Europe as well is now controlled by Soviet Russia. Naval bases were taken from Finland, the outlet to the Adriatic has been secured in Albania, attempts to dominate Azerbaijan in northern Iran were barely forestalled by the United States and other powers in 1945, Russian loans and "aid" have been granted to Afghanistan, and considerable gains have been made in the Far East since 1945. Czarist Russia knew the secret police, the collectivist principle in the management of village lands, and domestic tyranny of every sort, though these phenomena were less well developed and systematic in times past. Industrialization had begun on a significant scale in Old Russia and the government of Nicholas II tackled the illiteracy problem in earnest after 1900. Czarist Russia at least as far back as the sixteenth century thought of Western civilization as weak and decadent beside her own. The communists are of the same opinion, though not for the same reason. In his reckless determination to modernize and westernize his country, in his pitiless brutality and scorn for all humanitarian impulses, even in the savagery of his personal life, the communist dictator Stalin reminds one immediately of the Czars Peter the Great and Ivan the Terrible. So many and so obvious are the similarities between Old and New Russia that contemporary Russia has been defined variously as "an oriental despotism grown suddenly vigorous," and as "an efficient tyranny in contrast to the inefficient tyranny of the Czars." In fact, scholars have been arguing for years about which represents the real threat to the rest of the world: the international communist idea backed by Russian power, or Russian imperialism covered with communist varnish. In either case, one is reminded of the French proverb, "The more things change the more they remain the same."

Slowness of Change — More often than not when change does take place it comes slowly and gradually. Frequently the significance of a change is not appreciated until long after it has occurred. The history of warfare is replete with such instances. Alexander the Great, though always heavily outnumbered by his opponents, conquered most of the then known world in a decade. These successes were due primarily to a particular type of infantry formation called the phalanx and to a simple flanking maneuver not unlike an off-tackle play in football. The maneuver Alexander devised himself but the phalanx was the creation of a Theban general, Epimanondas, from whom Philip of Macedon, Alexander's father, had learned it decades earlier. For years it attracted little attention because the only wars in which Macedon and the small Greek city states were engaged were desultory civil conflicts. The Persians and other Asiatic opponents of Alexander were thus taken by surprise and easily defeated.

In 378 A.D. the Visigoths crushed a Roman army at Adrianople, a victory so decisive that the year 378 is sometimes designated as the end of the Roman Empire. The victory was due chiefly to the superiority of the Gothic heavy cavalry. Now the Visigoths had long possessed cavalry but in time past Roman infantry organization, training, and discipline had been so superior to that of the barbarian tribes that the latter's possession of cavalry, whatever its theoretical advantages over the Roman infantry legions, had been of no practical importance. The Romans, consequently, never attempted to devise any effective defense against cavalry. When the day came that the barbarians were better organized and disciplined, while the Romans had declined in these respects, the Roman infantry was helpless in the face of Gothic heavy cavalry charges.

The supremacy of cavalry in war lasted about 1000 years in Europe. It was first broken dramatically by the English longbowmen at Crecy in 1346. Here they systematically destroyed an army of heavily armored and mounted French knights before the knights were able to come close enough to use their swords and lances. Yet the longbow was not a new invention. Centuries earlier it had been used in border wars between the English and Welsh. Continental Europe paid little attention to these obscure skirmishes, however, and English armies seldom appeared south of the Channel. Hence the longbow came as a terrible surprise to the French. Perhaps most amazingly of all, the French knights learned remarkably little from Crecy for the English repeated the slaughter with the same weapon and in very similar circumstances at Poitiers in 1356 and again at Agincourt more than half a century later in 1415.

The development of the crossbow, longbow, and gunpowder (particularly the last), rendered armor useless since missiles propelled by these means could penetrate any plate armor — even that so thick and heavy that its wearer had to be hoisted onto his horse with a derrick. Against guns armor was worse than useless for the soft lead balls fired from muskets flattened against armor and then tore through it, inflicting a worse wound than if they had hit a man directly. These military facts of life were apparent in the fourteenth century in the case of the bows: in the case of the guns, in the first half of the sixteenth. Yet so conservative are men and so slowly does their thinking sometimes catch up with realities that the wearing of armor did not die out until the end of the Thirty Years War in 1648. One of the greatest soldiers of that war was King Gustavus Adolphus of Sweden. A considerable part of his success resulted from his taking most of the armor off his infantry and cavalry, thereby markedly increasing the speed with which men and horses could maneuver.

These examples indicate two things: 1) how a single change in weapons, tactics, or organization has often made possible sweeping military conquests, and 2) how tardily men sometimes realize the implications of such innovations and how long it takes them to devise effective counter-measures. Despite this, however, any study of war soon impresses the student with the timelessness of its major characteristics. Methods of waging war have been revolutionized successively by the phalanx, heavy cavalry, longbow, pike, gunpowder, machine gun, tank, airplane, and, presumably, nuclear bomb. No matter what the weapons employed however, the basic objective is always to defeat one's opponent. Whether wars are fought with swords or tanks there is no substitute for thorough training, high morale, and competent leadership. Be the weapons stones or A-Bombs no greater advantage can be gained over an enemy than to take him by surprise.

It is the same with most of man's major concerns. Though the physical conditions of human life have changed vastly through the centuries many of man's chief political and social problems have remained the same and appear no nearer final solution now than they were in the age of the ancient Greeks. How to combine efficiency in government with liberty for the individual? How to grant liberty to the individual without allowing him to infringe the liberty of others? How to give able men an incentive to invent, improve, and produce without allowing them to exploit their fellow men in the process? How to prevent destructive wars when nations hate, fear, and distrust one another? No matter what changes take place in man's environment these problems are changeless and eternal.

Theories About Historical Change — Many attempts have been made to trace patterns in history or to discern the nature and direction of historical change. Many ancient speculators, and the pessimistic sixteenth century political analyst Machiavelli, thought that history moved in cycles, each cycle substantially repeating the course of previous ones. A slight variation of this is the common view that the life of a nation or civilization closely resembles that of a man: e.g., first the Greeks and then the Romans passed through a period of youth when they worked hard, wrested lands from their neighbors, and established the foundations of their greatness. This was followed by their period of greatness, corresponding to an adult's middle life, when their cultures flourished, their armies were strong, their governments sound, and their wealth great. Then came their period of old age or decline in which their physical strength was allowed to ebb or was wasted in civil conflict, their wealth was dissipated, their governments grew slack and corrupt, and their empires were overrun by hardy, vigorous barbarian peoples.

Some have likened the course of history to the swinging of a pendulum, always striking out towards extremes and by that very effort constantly being brought back towards a center or compromise between the extremes. Many superficial examples can be cited to illustrate this conception. An obvious one concerns our own country. American governments from the Civil War to about 1900 were markedly conservative, regardless of the Party in power. The Administrations of Theodore Roosevelt, Taft, and especially Wilson, represented a swing of the pendulum in the direction of social legislation and the assumption by the government of a greater responsibility for the welfare of its citizens. In the 1920's, under Harding, Coolidge, and Hoover, the pendulum swung back to the Right again. Under the New Deal of the 1930's it swung far to the Left once more as Wilsonian trends were carried much further. Since the Second World War it has swung once more to the Right.

A somewhat more sophisticated version of this theory was the "dialectic" developed by the nineteenth century German philosopher Hegel. Hegel held that historical development takes place because any given situation or set of ideas which he called a "thesis," tends to produce its opposite or "antithesis." These two struggle, neither overcomes the other entirely, and the end result is a fusion of the two, a new thing which he called a "synthesis." This "synthesis" becomes, in effect, a new "thesis" which now engenders *its* "antithesis." From their conflict comes a new "synthesis." This new "synthesis" (really another new "thesis") engenders a new "antithesis," and so on. This hypothesis (much simplified here) is of interest chiefly because this "dialectic" was appropriated by Karl Marx and made one of the philosophical bases for modern communism.

Perhaps the most popular theory of historical change, at least among armchair philosophers in Western countries, is the idea of "progress": the belief that human history is the record of man's steady advancement in knowledge, wisdom, control over his environment, improvement of his institutions, and elevation of his ideals and conduct. This view was most popular about the turn of the twentieth century when it seemed clear that the spread of education, democratic institutions, and scientific knowledge was building a finer world. The depressions, wars, dictators, concentration camps, irrational political movements, and mass murders of the twentieth century have now made it quite clear that while knowledge may increase steadily, wisdom (the good use of knowledge) does not necessarily do so. It is sometimes alleged pessimistically that it is more likely that nuclear weapons will end all history than that there will be much more "progress." Whether or not this dire possibility ever becomes a reality, there is no gainsaying that "progress" has often been reversed in the past. Whole highly developed cultures, Assyrian, Egyptian, Minoan, and Mayan, to name a few, have vanished entirely and been replaced by obviously inferior civilizations.

Nobody can claim that he understands all history so thoroughly that he can discern perfectly the "pattern" that it follows, if, indeed, it has any pattern at all. It is precisely the weakness of every "grand philosophy" of history that the "philosophy" or explanation is conceived first and only afterward does its author select from the myriad of facts about the past whatever fits his theory. Whatever does not fit is ignored. A student's thought about the whole matter may be clarified, however, and without doing serious damage to the facts, if he likens the change and continuity in history to a river. The river begins as a tiny rivulet high in the mountains but grows steadily larger from the water fed into it by springs and tributary streams, the equivalent of new forces and ideas in history. The river is replete with currents, eddies, rapids, falls, pools, dams, obstructions, backwaters, and bayous; the counterparts of the wars, revolutions, dynastic shifts, inventions, and social, economic, and religious changes of history. The river assumes many different aspects; now rushing and dangerous, now calm, sometimes narrow, sometimes broad and placid: but nowhere does it stop completely, nowhere does it abruptly change character, nowhere does it cease to be water. Thus the course of history too.

CHAPTER IV

What Can We Really Know About History?

Virtually every teacher of history has had at some time or other the following experience: he is discussing the reliability of the historical source materials relating to some controverted question. As he finishes a hand shoots up and a student asks, "But which ones are reliable and which ones aren't?" Sometimes the discussion concerns varying interpretations of some historical event. At the conclusion the student asks, "Which one, now, is correct?" The attitude of the student here is neither unreasonable nor surprising for the human mind always seeks certitude. What the student must come to realize, however, is that certitude of the mathematical sort is not possible in history. There are many questions relating to past history that can never be answered; many disputes that can never be settled. Rarely, if ever, is a historical source so completely reliable that it may be taken at face value. Rarely is a source so untrustworthy that something cannot be learned from it.

History is man's memory of the past. The whole past can never be recalled and put into print because it consists of the infinite number of things which each person who ever lived has said, thought, and done. An infinite number of volumes would be required to record it. Historians select a few of these thoughts, words, and deeds that seem to have general significance, and these become history as we ordinarily think of it. Because men's ideas of what is significant change from time to time and because new knowledge frequently becomes available history is constantly being rewritten.

Here a distinction must be drawn. What actually happened in the past is done — settled — and no amount of research or re-interpretation can ever change it. The battle of Gettysburg was fought in a certain manner in a certain place on a certain day in 1863. Historians may write about it until the end of time but not the minutest detail of what *actually happened* will ever be changed on that account. But this is not the real problem. The crux of the matter is that, since we cannot re-live the past, what we know about it is largely what others tell us about it. It is what people in the past knew and thought, and especially what they wrote, about their own times.

History No Science — History is not a science. Natural scientists deal only with inanimate objects and chemical substances whose characteristics and reactions are known and invariable. If a chemist wishes to confirm a conclusion derived from a certain experiment he can always repeat the experiment — repeat it a hundred times if he chooses. The historian, however, cannot have the battle of Gettysburg fought over and over again in order that he may study it from every possible angle before writing his account of it. The best he can do is to re-read the written materials available and think about them again.

History is not like the biological sciences either. A biologist can observe animals, put them to tests, and dissect them, but the historian cannot resurrect Philip the Fair or Thomas Jefferson and do the same with them. He can only deal with written records about them. Moreover, the biological sciences seek information about one individual in order to generalize about a species; while history always studies the unique, the one situation for itself, since no other will ever be exactly like it. The substance of history is the deeds of men in time. But time never ceases to move, men never cease to act, and, because men are free agents, they are prone to do the most unlikely and unpredictable things. Thus history is not a science in the same sense as mathematics or biology. It is, rather, a kaleidoscope.

If history was a science we could predict the future in detail. Now prediction *is* possible in a limited sense. For one thing, the sameness of human nature causes the same general sort of situations to recur periodically. For another, any informed person can see that the persistence of oppression and tyranny will eventually produce revolt or that mutual dislike and constant rivalry between two peoples will sooner or later bring war. But this is plainly quite different from predicting what particular individuals or nations will do at particular future times. If one is determined to foretell the course of human affairs in detail he should consult astrologers, not historians.

The Raw Materials of History — A consideration of the materials from which history is derived and the manner in which they must be used will indicate the impossibility of attaining absolute certitude about the past. History is written largely from documents: private and official records, newspapers, diaries, letters, memoirs, annals, and other accounts penned by men recently or long since dead. All of these materials have defects and must be used with discretion.

Too Much Material — For the historian working in quite recent or contemporary history one of the major problems is the existence of an embarrassing superfluity of material. Books, newspapers, and magazines dealing with every conceivable subject are published in staggering numbers. Every governmental bureau and department, every local public agency, every business and labor organization, every society devoted to whatever cause, keeps records — usually in gigantic quantities. Practically every modern public figure in any field leaves behind him a vast correspondence and usually his memoirs as well. Some of this material is valuable and some is not. Some is readily accessible and much is widely scattered. The historian who regards this Mt. Everest of paper scarcely knows where to begin his researches and when to end them and start writing.

Too Little Material—With most ancient and medieval history the problem is exactly the reverse. Much *was* written in times past but the great bulk of it has failed to survive the ravages of water, wind, fire, rats, mice, invasion, conquest, and time. Thus the historian of the ancient or early medieval world has little raw material on which to base his work. He is forced to build part of his history from archaeological findings and part from old traditions, myths, and stories handed down orally from one generation to another. Anyone knows from experience how tales of the latter sort are likely to be changed or embroidered in the repeated retelling. Yet a good deal of early Norse history, to cite an example, is based on such tales and traditions written down centuries after the events they describe.

Often history is "filled out" by adding a great many inferences to a small core of facts. The inferences may be perfectly valid — and usually are — but they are not the same thing as documentary evidence. For instance, quite extensive accounts have been written of the lives of the early Germanic peoples. Virtually all the facts on which these are based come from one source, the Roman historian Tacitus. Normally a historian will accept and put into his own history only what is confirmed by two or three independent sources, but in this case one must either accept or reject Tacitus alone for his work is all that survives. Hence any account of the early Germans is Tacitus plus the inferences that a given writer draws from him.

Are Surviving Materials Typical?—A further complication is the fact that such materials as have survived may not be truly representative. It is quite possible, for example, that some 200 ancient writers might have written about a contemporary king but through the caprice of fate only the writings of his five harshest critics have survived. Some obvious prejudice can always be detected, of course, and the historian can often check suspect accounts against other writings, archaeological evidence, and his own common sense, but, still, who can doubt that in the case cited later generations would have a lower opinion of the king than the (unknown) facts warranted?

This example is not fanciful. A case quite similar to it concerns the Roman Emperor Tiberius, 14-37 A.D. Nearly all ancient writers whose works have survived agree that Tiberius was a monster in human form. They ascribe to him a character that seems close to unbelievable. They depict him at the age of eighty indulging in a variety of vices that seem even physically impossible. What is the reader to think here? Is he to conclude that all the ancient writers who were contemporaries of Tiberius were obviously ignorant or prejudiced and that we ought to strongly dilute their judgments, preferring those of historians who seldom stir from libraries and who write 1800 or 1900 years after the event? Is he to say, contrarily, that the ancients must be believed, no matter how incredible their accounts, because they knew of Tiberius at first hand while modern writers cannot; and that, anyway, there is no proof that modern writers are necessarily more impartial and judicious than their ancient counterparts? To be sure they are trained to be, but are they always? Plainly there is plenty of room for uncertainty about the whole matter.

Consider the problem in another way. Suppose that in the near future World War III breaks out between the Communist and Free Worlds and that it is waged with nuclear and bacteriological weapons. After a short time the only living humans left on earth are the inhabitants of the Fiji Islands. A few centuries hence some of them drift on a raft to the shores of what was once the United States. One of them is of a scholarly turn of mind and he decides to try to reconstruct the history of the twentieth century before the Third World War began. By the merest chance the only printed materials that have survived the holocaust are the files of the communist newspaper, *Daily Worker*. If our Fiji scholar is a shrewd man he will make allowances for what are obviously strongly opinionated accounts of world events but, even so, will his "history" of the twentieth century be likely to resemble the period we have lived through and know from experience? In the descriptions of factual happenings, perhaps, but hardly in the explanations advanced for the conduct of individuals, the policies of nations, or the general drift of world events. Suppose our Fiji historian decides to write a history of the New Deal in the United States and the only materials he can find are the files of the *Chicago Tribune* and the newspaper columns of Westbrook Pegler, two sources bitterly hostile to the Franklin D. Roosevelt Administration. Who would call the result "objective"? Yet things like this must have happened many times in the past. That certain ancient writings have been preserved and others lost or destroyed is largely accidental.

Frequently, too, the destruction of source materials is deliberate. Governments, political parties, business organizations, and private persons often destroy all or part of their records. Secret service agencies necessarily keep as few records as possible. Many documents or letters reflecting discredit upon a public figure have been deliberately destroyed. Needless to add, when only materials which show a person or an institution in a creditable light are permitted to survive the possibility of an accurate assessment becomes remote.

Deficiencies of Witnesses—The use of source materials is attended by many other difficulties related to this central one. Frequently we have little or no knowledge of the mental state of witnesses of events or of those who compile them. If the persons concerned were faulty in observation, or if they suffered from illusions, hallucinations, prejudices, or obsessions, these factors must have colored their testimony. Many people who composed the sources on which history is based were ignorant, incompetent, unscrupulous, partisan, careless, or simply not in a position to know much about what they wrote. Often such deficiencies can be detected from the tone or content of the writings themselves, but many times it is impossible to do more than guess about the reliability of a given account.

Forgeries—The historian's task has been complicated considerably by the devotion of many men to the deplorable habit of forging documents. Literally thousands of letters and other documents attributed to famous persons like Luther, Erasmus, Marie Antoinette, Washington, Lincoln, Franklin, Jefferson, and Napoleon have been forged because they could be sold, because somebody was anxious to enhance or destroy a reputation, or just to improve a story that seemed drab. Innumerable colorful anecdotes about celebrities have been invented to serve the last purpose. Some forgeries are designed to promote a cause. Perhaps the most famous in all history was the Donation of Constantine, a forgery composed to support various Papal claims against medieval temporal rulers. This document was fabricated in the eighth century and was accepted as genuine for nearly 400 years. After 1100 it came to be questioned increasingly: in the fifteenth century it was shown conclusively to be spurious. The celebrated Protocols of the Elders of Zion was forged to "prove" that the Jews had an elaborate plan to dominate the world. Minnesota's famous Kensington Stone, which describes a fourteenth century Norse expedition to that state, is thought by many experts to be a forgery.

There are elaborate techniques that can be employed to detect forgeries but success cannot always be guaranteed. For example, the historical reputation of Mary Stuart, a sixteenth century Queen of Scotland, will almost certinly never be settled beyond reasonable doubt due to the famed Casket Letters. These letters, purportedly from Mary to the Earl of Bothwell, whom she later married, were supposedly discovered in a small silver casket belonging to a servant of Bothwell. Their authenticity has never been definitely established. If they are genuine then Mary was certainly implicated in the murder of her previous husband, Lord Darnley. If they are fabrications she deserves rather a better niche in history than she is usually accorded.

Frequently source materials are altered in other ways well short of forgery. Many an editor has softened or sharpened the wording of a passage or deleted parts of a narrative without notifying his readers. Innumerable writers have copied from others, passing on errors in the originals and adding new ones of their own. In modern times much that is purportedly written by public figures is actually produced by "ghost writers." To determine exactly what belongs to the mind and pen of each party, and to tell with what accuracy the "ghost" has reproduced the ideas of his employer, is a nice problem.

Bias—Much history has been distorted by the prejudices of both the compilers of source material and professional historians. A comparison of present day communist and noncommunist accounts of world affairs provides a good illustration. People in the Free World take it for granted that communists never write an objective account of anything because, in the first place, they put themselves in an intellectual strait-jacket by their acceptance of Marxist dogma and, in the second, they must always defend and apologize for communist dictatorships. Thus their writings are mere propaganda, worth reading only to see what attitudes communist governments are assuming at the moment. Communist publicists and historians reply that theirs must necessarily be the only accurate, objective accounts. Since non-Marxists do not understand the laws of historical development (as revealed by Karl Marx and refined by Lenin, Stalin, and other disciples), noncommunist writings on any period past or present cannot be anything but superficial and full of errors.

Plots—Serious difficulties arise whenever a historian has reason to believe that a plot was a significant factor in a given situation. Plots are innumerable. Every coup d'etat that overthrows a government is the result of a plot. For every such scheme that succeeds there are usually several that fail and some that are abandoned by the plotters because they lose their nerve or circumstances change. These we sometimes learn about afterward when it becomes safe to make the revelations. Often we never learn of them because plotters are not in the habit of leaving filing cabinets full of records for historians to peruse at their leisure. To consider a common example, any reasonable, informed person knows that communists plot constantly because all ex-communists say so, the techniques have been described many times, and the results of communist plots are plain for all to see. Yet no written records of these activities are kept. What is the historian to do in such cases? If he takes the narrow view "no records, no history" he is going to consciously tell less than the whole truth. If he decides to deal with plots in his narrative he must resort to some amount of speculation in the absence of tangible documentary evidence.

Innate Deficiency In Various Kinds of Materials—Many types of historical raw materials and written history have weaknesses which are peculiar to the nature of the source and which the historian must consider when using them.

1) *Biography*—One such is biography. Many people love biography and, in fact, develop an interest in history largely as a result of reading biographies of famous persons. This is in no way surprising or disreputable. It is men, after all, who make history, and it is not possible to understand the past without understanding the psychology of the chief persons who have shaped it. Good biography is just as sound and just as valuable as any other type of historical writing.

Yet history is easily distorted by biographers. To begin with, why does one person write a biography of another? Usually because he has a keen interest in his subject and strong feelings about him. More often than not he will be an admirer of his subject, though many biographies have been written to expose what the author regarded as the infamy of another person. A trained and conscientious biographer will attempt to be fair and factual, but it is deceptively easy, if one has sympathy for his subject, to emphasize the subject's virtues and strengths and to minimize or suppress his mistakes and weaknesses. Occasionally biographers become so infatuated with their subjects that they abandon their critical faculties altogether. Biographies written by persons of the same religious, political, or party affiliation as their subjects are not infrequently of this type. "Campaign biographies" are notoriously so. Sometimes a biography is "authorized"; that is, the subject or, if he is deceased, his family, allows the biographer access to correspondence and other materials on condition that a veto is retained over statements the biographer may make in his book. In these ways many half-truths and falsehoods creep into history, to be repeated in secondary works for generations afterward.

The same thing frequently happens when a biographer sets out to "expose" or "debunk" some historical personage. The subject may never entirely recover from deliberate or inadvertent slanders so inflicted. It is generally accepted by present day scholars, for example, that the famous Borgia family of the Renaissance, King Philip II of Spain, and Richard III of England, have been unduly maligned by past writers.

Finally, it is easy for biography to distort historical accuracy for a reason that has nothing to do with the frailties of biographers. It is the nature of a biography to make its subject everywhere the center of things; to describe every idea, event, and development in terms of its relationship to the principal figure in the book. Real life is just not like this.

2) *Memoirs*—Memoirs are a valuable source of history because they are usually written by statesmen, soldiers, or other public figures who have had a good deal to do with making history. They must be used with caution, however, for they are commonly written to justify their authors. Memoirists want to portray their ideas, deeds, and careers in the best possible light. Moreover, memoirs are normally written in old age, many years after the events they describe. If the author has kept a diary or careful notes throughout his life he may be able to describe quite accurately his ideas and feelings decades earlier. If he has not, if at the age

of sixty or seventy or eighty he has to rely on his memory to describe events and thoughts when he was twenty, thirty, or forty, the pitfalls are obvious. Let the reader ask himself, "How many conversations of five years ago, one year ago, one month ago, can *I* recall accurately? How exactly can *I* reconstruct my state of mind with regard to this or that matter of four or five years ago?"

3) *Diplomatic Correspondence*—One of the best sources for political history is diplomatic correspondence. But it is a two-edged sword. The formal reports of diplomats are notoriously full of lies, half-truths, and sentiments which the diplomat or his government may wish to get into public circulation. Private dispatches, intended only for the eyes of political superiors, often tell quite a different story. Diplomatic correspondence is easily misinterpreted too. It is full of conventional expressions that do not mean what they appear to mean. Worse, the conventions change from time to time. This is not much of a problem in the mid-twentieth century because ideological hostility is so fierce and undisguised in our time — and the prospect of war has grown so appalling — that heads of state often exchange insults in regular diplomatic correspondence without fear of provoking anything worse than a similar barrage of words from the enemy state. This was not the case in times past. In the nineteenth century a note sent from one European chancellery to another might contain some such phrase as "His Majesty's Government must reserve the right to deal with this matter as later circumstances indicate." The real meaning of such a seeming innocuous phrase was that the second government was being warned that the situation could lead to war.

This general state of affairs is, of course, well known to scholars who work in the field of political and diplomatic history, and suitable allowances are made, but it is still easy for those writing long after the event and perhaps not completely familiar with the conventions of an age to misinterpret.

4) *Propaganda*—Governments, organizations, and private persons have always striven to present a favorable picture of themselves to the world but the problems posed by this for the writer and reader of history were incomparably smaller before the age of general literacy, mass circulation newspapers and magazines, radio, and television. Most propaganda is not harmful or packed with lies, as is sometimes mistakenly thought, though of course it may be so. It is, however, always an organized effort to influence public opinion in some way. It never attempts to tell the whole truth

about anything but rather to leave a certain impression in the mind of the reader or listener. The course of modern history has been strongly affected by propaganda of various types. Allied propaganda, centered about Wilson's "Fourteen Points" and a proposed "League of Nations," certainly hastened the Allied victory over Germany and Austria-Hungary in World War I. Less happily, it gave rise to immoderate expectations of a finer and more peaceful world afterward — expectations that proved illusory and bedevilled international politics for a generation. Clever propaganda in the 1930's secured for Adolf Hitler the solid support of most German people and weakened the wills of neighboring nations to resist Nazi aggression. In American domestic politics the propaganda effort of the Democrats to depict the Republicans as the Party of Big Business, Depressions, and callous disregard for the "little man" has enjoyed considerable success, as election results since 1932 have shown. A Republican propaganda effort to link the Democrats with communism had a briefer and more limited success in the decade after World War II.

The Historian's Function—Much historical writing needs to be read critically merely because past chroniclers and historians had a different view of their function than do their modern counterparts. A modern historian trained in a reputable graduate school tries to put into his works "the facts, the whole facts, and nothing but the facts" — nothing further, that is, than "the most reasonable and meaningful interpretation of the facts." Like all ideas, this one is never attained perfectly for historians are as fallible as other men. Nonetheless, the bulk of contemporary historical writing is as accurate and impartial as can reasonably be expected.

This was not always true in times past; not because our ancestors were less honorable or possessed feebler intellects than we but because they had a different view of the historian's task. For centuries history was regarded as a branch of literature. The chief concern of the writer of history was to amuse his readers by telling a lively story or to edify them by pointing lessons in his works. Much "history" was based on secondary accounts, hearsay, memoirs, rumors, commonly accepted stories, and mere imagination. Little or no attempt was made to investigate carefully original records, to compare texts and sources, and to distinguish rigorously between provable fact and mere common opinion. These traditions lasted a long time. As late as 1700 the English litterateur, Laurence Eachard, decided to write a history of England from the time of

Julius Caesar onward. He openly avowed that it was not becoming that a great lord of letters like himself should spend time rummaging around in a lot of crude monkish records. Rather, he said, he would take what seemed worthy of preservation from his predecessors and mould it into his own history. A generation later Voltaire, in some ways the ablest historian of his age, wrote expansively about all sort of subjects and events without knowing the languages necessary for basic research about them. He relied on published secondary works, a few translations, conversations with persons who possessed some first hand knowledge, and a large amount of "reasoning" and pure imagination.

History has also been distorted by persons who write to promote some religious, political, national, or other cause. These persons usually begin their labors with a set of preconceptions and then twist the facts until the desired message is wrung from them. We are all familiar with "patriotic" histories in which one's own countrymen, led by heroes, promenade grandly through the "glorious" pages. Like television cowboys, they right wrongs, struggle for freedom, and repeatedly save the country from rascally enemies and "foreigners."

The ecclesiastical chroniclers of the Middle Ages frequently proceeded in a similar manner. They interpreted everything that happened in the world in terms of God's designs for men and consequently forced all events into an artificial mould. When they had occasion to write a *life* of some saint they often suppressed any sort of weakness the person might have had and dwelt entirely upon his virtues. Not infrequently prodigies were invented to make the saint seem even more holy and worthy of emulation than was actually the case. In doing this the writers were not being consciously dishonest. It simply did not occur to them that their function was to display the bare truth. They thought it their business to teach, to edify, to persuade men to live better lives, and to lead them towards God by holding before them models of dazzling sanctity and heroism.

Mechanical Errors—History composed from written documents may sometimes be distorted by unavoidable human and mechanical errors. Documents relating to ancient and medieval history are extremely scarce. In many cases original documents have long since been lost or destroyed and all that is left are copies and copies of copies. Even if the originals still exist they are usually locked in rare book rooms of museums and libraries, very likely on a different continent. Thus what the historian normally uses are copies and copies of translations. The possibilities of mechanical errors creeping in are endless. No human being can copy entire books, as medieval monks did for centuries, and have them exactly like the originals in every minute detail. It is easy to mistake words, to skip lines, to be unable to decipher the handwriting of the original and to "guess at" what it was likely to have been, and so on. By the time this has been done several times by different persons a great many errors have usually crept in. With modern materials the question of typing errors arises.

More serious are changes of meaning introduced by translations. Every language has shades of meaning impossible to duplicate exactly in other languages. Even the most able and conscientious translator can often only approximate the meaning of the original. In the historic past many translators have gravely altered meanings in materials they have handled. Suppose a given document was written originally in Hebrew. Then it was translated into Greek, the Greek translation was then rendered into Aramaic, and the Aramaic version was then translated into Latin. In each case the translation was done by a different unknown person and in the process everything but the final Latin version was lost. Who can doubt that it was probably different in many particulars from the original Hebrew?

Other Sources of Information—Not all historical knowledge comes from written records. A great deal can be reconstructed from monuments, inscriptions, ruins, coins, seals, and other artifacts. From them the historian not only secures much information about the past but he is better able to assess the meaning and worth of written records. Studies of this sort, however, are no magical remedy for all the defects of documents, for these materials themselves require much "interpreting" before they become meaningful and these interpretations are often changed as more information becomes available. Finally, the anthropologist and the student of ancient or rare language can often provide much inferential guidance for the historian, but again the question of accurate interpretation arises.

The Historian's Bias—Lastly, perfect certitude in history is impossible to achieve because even the most carefully trained and conscientious historian is still moved by his personal feelings. Nothing indicates more clearly the dissimilarity of history and science than the fact that the historian has an *attitude* about his subject matter while the natural scientist does not. Every historian has political, social, national, religious, and economic beliefs. He admires some human traits and human types and thinks others despicable. He regards some historical developments as constructive and praiseworthy and others the reverse. These preferences are bound to color both his selection of materials (for he cannot include everything) and the use he makes of them. A mathematician, by contrast, does not admire plus signs and detest minus signs. A physicist does not feel kindly towards velocity but averse to acceleration.

A distinguished living historian, Herbert Butterfield, refers to the "magnet in men's minds" which leads them to draw out of raw historical materials just those facts and examples that fit the shape of the story as they conceived it beforehand; that confirm all their prejudices; that shore up long accepted views; that illuminate maxims already in their minds. The same predilection is, of course, well nigh universal among the general public too. A lifelong Republican and an admirer of Franklin D. Roosevelt each read an academic history of the New Deal. Does each put down the book with the feeling that he has gained a new appreciation of the reasonableness of the other's position? Occasionally, yes, but much more often each merely grows more deeply convinced of the iniquity of the other's views and learns a few new arguments to support his own.

Consider the book you are now reading. If it had been written by someone else it would still have been the same sort of book and its message would have been similar but it certainly would have been different in many particulars. Another author would have chosen different examples to make some of its points; parts of it he probably would have left out entirely; other parts would have been expanded; some things which are not in this book at all would have been added; and some matters discussed here would have been interpreted differently. So it is with all history. It has been well said that "The only completely unbiassed historian is . . . the Recording Angel; and doubtless he has convictions which to Satan . . . would seem prejudices."[1]

This is not a plea for no interpretations in the writing of history. That is impossible and absurd. History has to be interpreted to have any meaning. The difference, in practice, is not between an

---

1. Allan Nevins, *The Gateway to History*, pp. 41-42.

interpretation or philosophy of history and the absence of one but between a sensible philosophy and a ridiculous or pernicious one. The thing for the student to remember is that everybody has one of *some* kind, be it sensible or not.

What Can We Know?—By now the reader is probably disconsolate, disgusted, thoroughly confused, or all three. He may well think that history is such a hopeless jumble of uncertainties and subjective judgments that the late Henry Ford was right when he once declared, "history is bunk." He should take heart. Things are not as bad as they seem. All of the foregoing discussion is designed to demonstrate one truth: that from the nature of man and the nature of the materials with which he has to deal, the historian cannot achieve certitude of the type the mathematician possesses when he says that the area of a circle equals πr^2 or that the chemist has when he says that hydrogen and oxygen when mixed in the proportion of two to one will yield water. It does not mean that the historian cannot achieve relative certitude; that he cannot attain the kind of certitude that all of us accept without question every day of our lives.

Skepticism has its place but it must be guided by common sense. In everyday life we all take for granted most things we read or are told by others. How else, in fact, could we live? How could chemistry, medicine, physics, astronomy, or any other science ever progress if each scientist rigorously refused to accept any information reported to him by his fellows unless he could personally verify it by experiment? It is equally reasonable to believe what we read about the past provided that we do not let our critical faculty go to sleep in the process. Think for a moment of Abraham Lincoln. He is commonly held to have been a great American President. Is a man foolish and credulous because he believes this without having personally investigated every aspect of Lincoln's personal life and public career? Suppose everyone acted on the principle of refusing assent to any proposition not personally investigated. The world would be a bedlam. We would all starve to death in our feverish search for absolute certitude.

There is a vast difference between skepticism about facts and about their interpretation. What sane man doubts the existence of England, even though he has not been there personally and even though he may entertain erroneous ideas about the place? Who doubts that George Washington existed, commanded the Colonial Army in the American Revolution, crossed the Delaware, and was

President? Though we were not there ourselves innumerable men who were have testified to the truth of these allegations and a vast array of written materials concerning them survive. Only a lunatic would disregard it.

Where skepticism is legitimate is not when one reads of Washington crossing the Delaware but when he reads that on such and such an occasion Washington was thinking this, planning that, estimating the possibility of something else, or convinced of this or that. Here certitude can be *probable,* but nothing more. It is true that human nature is much the same at all times; that many human attitudes are generally uniform and predictable. Parents generally love and protect their children; a man will normally defend his possessions with tenacity and vigor; a person of recognized integrity normally does not commit shocking crimes; a man commonly prefers members of his own tribe, race, party, or religion to others; most men are moved to some degree by ambition, vanity, and love of power; and so on. The historian knows all this and if he is familiar with Washington's character he may *reasonably infer* that Washington was thinking or planning this or that on the occasion. But he cannot *know beyond question* for what person understands completely all *his own* thoughts and motives for contemplating or undertaking a certain action? How much less certain must he be about those of another person? How much less certain still about those of someone long since dead? Nobody can ever get inside the mind of another. Thus judgments about the ideas, plans, and intentions of historical figures are only inferences; quite accurate ones most of the time, no doubt, but never beyond question.

History is full of instances where the *deeds* of men are clear but their *motives* are not. There is no dispute about the facts of Alexander the Great's conquests but there are two theories about Alexander the man. The first is that he was a genius who set out, consciously and deliberately, to spread Greek civilization over the then known world. The second is that he was a madman (albeit one with military gifts) ; an egomaniac who thought only of conquest. According to the second view the spread of Greek civilization was an incidental by-product of the conquests. Most of the relatively little that we know about Alexander supports the first interpretation but one can never be certain because it will never be possible to get inside the mind of Alexander and find out what he thought and planned.

A more recent and complex case is that of the famous seventeenth century soldier of fortune, Wallenstein. Wallenstein was born in Bohemia. He fought in the employ of the Hapsburg Holy Roman Emperor Ferdinand II in the Thirty Years War; though he was so independent of his employer that he raised, outfitted, fed, and paid his army out of his own resources. Ferdinand was so fearful of Wallenstein's growing and uncontrollable power that he eventually had his great mercenary assassinated in 1634. Most of Wallenstein's papers have disappeared in the course of time and historians have never been able to agree on his ultimate intentions. Some hold that he planned to displace the Hapsburgs and make himself Holy Roman Emperor. Others think it more likely that he aspired to be the Richelieu of the Empire, to turn the hundreds of scattered German states into a unified national state ruled by Ferdinand II with himself (Wallenstein) as chief minister. Some insist that he cared nothing for the Germanies: that his ultimate design was to create an independent and enlarged Bohemia. It is known that shortly before Wallenstein's death Cardinal Richelieu, the virtual ruler of France and an opponent of the Hapsburgs in the Thirty Years War, offered to set him up as king of an independent Bohemia, in return for which Wallenstein was to desert the Hapsburgs. Wallenstein was killed before reaching any decision about the offer. There are reasons for suspecting that Wallenstein had proposed to King Gustavus Adolphus of Sweden that the pair join forces and divide central Europe between them. He may have been preparing to desert to the Swedes when he was killed. Thus while the *facts* of Wallenstein's life are clear, nobody really knows what his *intentions* were and doubtless no one ever will know for the designs were locked in his mind and went to the grave with him.

While deficiencies in source materials present obstacles to the searcher for truth, these are not insurmountable. Many writers in times past may have been uncritical by modern standards but where it has been possible to check their credibility from other sources the great majority of them have been found to be trustworthy in essentials if not always in details. This is often the case even with myths and legends. For centuries the Homeric account of the Trojan War was thought to be mythical but in the nineteenth century archaeological excavations by Schliemann and others established the existence of Troy and the substantial accuracy of the tale related in Homer's *Iliad*. Ought we to be surprised? Not really, for, after all, men normally tell the truth as they see it, particularly when they have no motive for not doing so. When ancient writers were biased or had some ulterior motive this is often obvious from the tone of their writings. Anyway, what modern writer is entirely free from these faults? We do not refuse to believe things written by contemporary writers merely because we happen to know that not every one of them is simultaneously deeply learned, wholly impartial, and infallibly correct in his judgments. Suppose four serious but quite different American magazines, *The Reporter, National Review, America,* and *Christian Century,* print articles on some controversial subject. The accounts and judgments will be different in many ways, perhaps drastically different in some, but anyone familiar with the magazines will expect this and make allowances for it and will not think any of the writers liars, fools, or charlatans. It is the same when reading history. A knowledge of the reputation, background, and affiliations of the historian or the author of a source material is most enlightening, and the student ought to acquire it if he can, but whatever it might be it does not in itself invalidate the man's statements or judgments. If we know that the author of a *History of the United States Steel Corporation* was hired by the company to write the book we will read it more warily than if we lacked this information but it does not follow that everything in the book will be false or wilfully distorted.

The Re-Writing of History—History is constantly being rewritten. Does this prove that we really do not know much about the past? No. History is rewritten for three basic reasons: 1) because new information becomes available, 2) to weed out inaccurate, misleading, biased, or false statements or conclusions, and 3) because men's intellectual interests change and new problems arise which provide new views of the past.

1) *New Information*—History must frequently be rewritten and its interpretation changed because new knowledge becomes available. The discovery of the Rosetta Stone by Champollion in 1799 made it possible to decipher Egyptian hieroglyphics and thereby to add vastly to our knowledge of ancient Egypt. The rewriting of that history naturally followed. It has long been known that a well-developed and thriving civilization existed on the island of Crete before 1000 B.C. Not until 1952-3, however, was anyone able to decipher the Cretan language. Now that this has been accomplished there is every indication that when scholars have completed their studies of Minoan (Cretan) written materials much of the early history of ancient Greece will have to be revised. It is already clear

that the Minoans influenced the Greeks in various ways hitherto unsuspected. Recent excavations in Turkey suggest that parts of it may have been settled as early or earlier than the valleys of the Tigris and Euphrates rivers. If these intimations prove correct portions of the ancient history of western Asia will have to be rewritten. The Dead Sea Scrolls discovered in Palestine since World War II have already produced a number of books and some spirited controversies among scholars about problems relating to the early history of Christianity.

In modern times a great deal more became known about many episodes in the past when the Vatican Archives were opened during the pontificate of Leo XIII, 1878-1903. The details, though seldom the main lines, of diplomatic history have to be altered from time to time since governments generally refuse to make diplomatic records available to historians until many years after the events with which they are concerned. Similarly, statesmen ordinarily write their memoirs in old age, long after the more important events in which they had a part. The fact that historical knowledge is incomplete does not mean, however, that it is not reasonably sure. The Governments of Russia, Great Britain, and the United States will probably not release all their records relating to World War II for another thirty or forty or fifty years, but nobody claims on this account that our knowledge of the causes, course, and results of that conflict is not substantially correct. It is merely incomplete.

This condition is not peculiar to history. It exists in every field of study. The ideas and discoveries of Newton, Planck, Einstein, and others have successively shaken the basic concepts of physics far more radically than has ever been the case in the writing of history. Three physics textbooks, written in 1880, 1920, and 1960 would bear small resemblance to one another. Yet nobody says it is useless to study physics. The most fundamental idea in ancient and medieval astronomy, that the earth is the center of the universe and the other heavenly bodies revolve around it, was discarded in the sixteenth and seventeenth centuries, but this did not cause men to abandon the study of astronomy. We do not refuse to go to a doctor when sick merely because we know that in the past many medical ideas and practices were injurious or absurd. Medical knowledge even now is extremely imperfect but this does not prevent doctors from curing many ills and trying to remedy all of them.

In man's search for knowledge complete victory will never be achieved. Yet added knowledge in any field clarifies situations that were formerly vague, corrects errors, and provides the bases for new advances. The fact that not everything is known about history, or that not all historians agree about the meaning of what is known, is no argument for refusing to study history or for saying that one theory is as good as the next. It is an argument for studying more, and more carefully, and trying to come as close to the truth as possible.

2) *Correction of Errors*—Much history is rewritten to correct inaccuracies or biases in past accounts. This is a pressing necessity in the case of highly controversial episodes in the past: revolutions, religious upheavals, or sweeping economic and social changes. For generations after the Protestant Reformation of the sixteenth century men wrote in zeal, anger, or disgust to justify Catholicism and condemn Protestantism, or the reverse, or to demonstrate that all the protagonists in that tumultuous century were fanatics and fools. Centuries had to pass before tempers cooled sufficiently to allow the religious history of those times to be written with something like objectivity and fairness to all parties. Now, happily, no serious Catholic historian pretends that the sixteenth century Protestant leaders were a pack of scoundrels perversely bent on destroying unblemished Catholicism. No Protestant historian who commands respect or attention depicts the Protestant leaders as a band of saintly heroes nobly assaulting an international colossus of crime, corruption, and superstition.

The French Revolution of 1789-1799 has produced whole libraries of books. The Old Regime has been praised and condemned from every possible angle. Scores of historians have endeavored to prove that the revolution was "caused" primarily by the weakness of Louis XVI, or by the ideas of the eighteenth century philosophers, or the bankruptcy of the French Government, or the injustices rampant in French society, or even plots by Freemasons! Such major revolutionary figures as Danton, Robespierre, Mirabeau, and Marat have been lauded and denounced. Republican historians have tried to demonstrate that the Revolution's products were freedom, equality, and progress. Royalist writers have labored to prove that its products were militarism, nationalist fanaticism, social chaos, and ultimately, modern dictatorship. All these disputes are not yet settled but most twentieth century books on the French Revolution are more moderate in tone and less concerned to hold strongly to one point of view than those written in the nineteenth.

It is the same with writing about the American Revolution or the Civil War. As any controversial episode recedes into the past it is seen in truer perspective. At first everyone who has an interest to serve writes his version of it. Then detailed research is undertaken by generations of scholars increasingly removed from the happenings themselves. All the opinionated versions are compared and the obvious errors, biases, and lies weeded out. The rewriting begins and a century or two later a fairer and better balanced account usually emerges.

3) *Changing Interests*—Changing circumstances cause variations in intellectual interests, and these, in turn, color the writing of history. It is not that facts change but that our interest in them changes and the vantage point from which we view them changes. New problems arise in the present which cause us to become interested in past men and episodes that have not heretofore attracted our attention. Since not *all* facts can ever be put in one book or in any 1,000,000 books what *is* put in reflects what any given generation thinks is significant.

Our ancestors used to think that the doings of kings and governments were the most important things that transpired. Consequently, history used to be mostly "past politics." Eighteenth and nineteenth century writers, however, broadened its scope. Voltaire wrote history primarily in terms of ideas. Montesquieu, and later Buckle, wove much information about climate and geography into their histories. Adam Smith and innumerable disciples emphasized economic factors. In the twentieth century historians endeavor to portray every aspect of the civilizations about which they write.

Consider a specific case. In times past virtually everyone took war for granted and thus paid little attention to persons who worked out schemes to insure universal peace. In the last century, however, and particularly since 1917, great numbers of people have come increasingly to believe that it is necessary to prevent wars and that it is possible to do so. Accordingly, such figures as Hugo Grotius (1625) and the Abbe Saint Pierre (1711-1713) who devised peace-keeping schemes are now mentioned more often and at greater length in books than they used to be. It is not that the men have changed or that their ideas are of greater intrinsic importance; merely that we have become more interested in them and they seem more important to us.

The spread of democratic ideas and institutions since 1776 has led to a widespread interest in tracing democratic practices and experiments back into the past. Predictably, some zealots have "gone overboard," in this case professing to discover the germs of modern British and American governmental practices among the Germanic tribesmen of the first centuries A.D. In the 1920's and 1930's there was a pronounced tendency to interpret history in terms of economic changes and rivalries, a condition which derived in considerable measure from the impression made on men's minds by the communist experiment in Russia and the world-wide depression of the early 1930's. The conviction has grown rapidly in recent decades that the Middle Ages were much more important than used to be thought and that the modern world has grown more directly out of them than out of Greek and Roman antiquity. This belief is reflected in the increasingly careful and respectful treatment accorded the Middle Ages in textbooks and European Survey courses. Any number of similar examples could be cited.

Finally, let us sum up by considering just how history is written. Normally, a considerable number of scholars are working in any one field at any given time. Each searches for materials, weighs his findings, evaluates, considers, questions, speculates, and then writes. Each reads and criticizes what his fellows have written, pointing out any errors into which they may have fallen. In the end the result is not absolute certitude about every detail but as close an approximation to the truth as men are ever apt to achieve when they must describe the deeds and intentions of other men.

The recording of history may be compared to a trial by jury. Some of the evidence leads to quite definite, certain conclusions. Some of it consists of a converging series of probabilities which amount to moral certitude. Some of it gives rise to interesting speculations and hypotheses but, since proof is lacking, they must be ruled out. The jury weighs, considers, and comes to its conclusion. The result is generally acclaimed as just and reasonable. There the matter rests unless someone turns up new evidence or demonstrates some error in the trial.

In actuality the historian is in a better position than a judge and jury to be just, fair, and certain because there is no time pressure on him. He can study more thoroughly and deliberate longer and more calmly before making his decisions. He therefore has a better chance of being right.

CHAPTER V

Is History the Work of Great Men?

The student of history is perennially troubled by the problem of causation. Why do things change? What is the most important factor or factors in producing historical change? Why did the Roman Empire fall? What caused the French Revolution? Can World War I be ascribed to essentially one factor, one country, one man? Questions of this sort pose themselves at every turn in history. Innumerable attempts have been made to answer them. Some of the proffered answers will be discussed at length in later chapters but here it is essential to first draw a distinction between remote and immediate causation.

Remote and Immediate Causes—Most complex or important events are precipitated by some happening that ought more properly to be called an occasion than a cause since it is usually quite trivial in comparison with the events that follow from it. The assassination of the Austrian Archduke Franz Ferdinand on June 28, 1914 "caused" the First World War in the sense that it set off a train of events that culminated in war a month later. It was the immediate pretext or occasion for the war. The remote and much more important causes of the war, however, had little to do with Franz Ferdinand. German militarism, French desire to regain Alsace-Lorraine, the Anglo-German naval race, Austro-Russian rivalry in the Balkans, and the determination of the German and Hungarian peoples in the Austro-Hungarian Empire to keep the Empire's other ethnic groups in a subordinate position, more truly "caused" the war. It is quite likely that these factors would have produced a major European war at *some* time had Franz Ferdinand never lived. The latter's assassination merely provided a pretext for Austria-Hungary to try to settle old scores with Serbia in a way that other European powers refused to tolerate. Thus war resulted at this particular time instead of at some other.

The immediate "cause" of the fall of the Roman Empire appears to have been its invasion by the barbarians, but if one considers the phenomenon more closely it is soon evident that the barbarian invaders would have been repulsed had not Roman society already decayed to the point of collapse. Many different explanations have been advanced to account for this disintegration: moral corruption of the populace, overtaxation, overpopulation, the decline in the morale and efficiency of the Roman army following from the introduction into it of barbarian soldiers, soil exhaustion, climatic changes, lack of a set rule of succession to the throne, the decay of Roman economic life, and others. Historians have never been able to agree which of these considerations was the most important element in Rome's fall but all of them contributed to it in some degree. Certainly all of them taken collectively were more truly the "cause" of the decline of Rome than were the barbarian invasions.

These two considerations, then, the reader should keep in mind as he reads the rest of this book: the immediate cause of an event is not the same or, usually, nearly as important as the basic causes; and almost any complex or important development will be the result of several forces or factors. The more important of these factors will now be considered individually and in some detail.

The Individual In History—The importance of the individual man in determining the course of history has long been the subject of heated argument. The nineteenth century historian, Thomas Carlyle, thought that men of genius were the prime movers of the world's affairs and that history was, indeed, the sum of innumerable individual biographies. The ordinary person tends to accept a similar view. He thinks of politics, government, warfare, and other human activities, primarily in terms of men prominent in these fields rather than in terms of ideas or institutions. If something goes awry in the world his natural tendency is to blame some man for it — Roosevelt, Truman, Hitler, Khrushchev. As a reaction against this excessive personalization of events many historians have gone to the opposite extreme and denied the importance of the individual, ascribing change, instead, to ideas, geography, economic conditions, or other impersonal factors. In their view, the individual man is not the master of these forces but is largely swept along by them. The truth of the matter lies between these two extremes.

It is absurd to deny the importance of great men in history when the significance of the individual is a matter of common experience in everyday life. Who thinks it of no consequence what partner he has in business? What congregation is indifferent to its pastor? What owner of a baseball team thinks one manager is as good as another? What manager is unaware of the difference between the "winning ballplayer" type and the type who tends to "choke up in the clutch"? What teacher gives all students the same grade on the ground that they are equally intelligent and worthy? Any organization, private or public, civilian or military, past or present, functions more efficiently when headed by an able man and staffed by capable personnel.

The importance of the individual is evident in many other ways too. Most of the great ideas, deeds, and inventions that have successively changed the human environment have been the work of exceptionally talented and determined individuals. Who can reasonably claim that Aristotle, Shakespeare, Pascal, Newton, Beethoven, Napoleon, Bismarck, and Edison were ordinary men: mere products of their environment? The opposite is obvious: they were men of exceptional talent whose ideas, works, and example strongly influenced subsequent times. The course of history has always been affected markedly by the pride, ambition, and determination of individual kings, soldiers, and prophets. Men have always done many things merely because they were resolved to triumph, to "be first," to impose their ways on others rather than suffer the ways of others to be imposed on them. A mountain climber was once asked why he risked his life to scale a particularly challenging peak. He replied, "Because it is there." This spirit has always been part of the human makeup. In countries where kings or dictators rule their realms personally and without effective constitutional checks history can be changed decisively by the ambition or caprice of a few men — or of only one. In the Middle Ages and early modern times wars were often fought for personal, even frivolous, reasons. Kings frequently went to war to gain prestige for themselves or their dynasties, or just for amusement, rather than to serve any interest of their peoples. The classic example is Charles XII of Sweden, 1697-1718. Uninterested in government, money, physical comfort, display, or intellectual pursuits, Charles had one consuming passion — war. From his accession to the throne of Sweden at the age of fifteen until his death on the battlefield two decades later he thought of nothing but fighting and spent all his time planning and conducting campaigns against his neighbors. The money and manpower drained from Sweden to support these mad projects left the nation exhausted and reduced to the status of a third-rate power.

The personal ambtion of Charles the Bold of Burgundy had even worse results for that fifteenth century state. In 1470 Burgundy was probably the richest state in Europe. Ten years later, because its quixotic ruler thought himself destined to be a great conqueror, it had been erased from the map. Charles the Bold raised an expensive but militarily obsolete feudal army which was destroyed by Swiss pikemen in the battles of Grandson, Morat, and Nancy in 1476 and 1477. Charles was killed at Nancy and his lands were divided between France and the Holy Roman Empire. Who can say that the personality and ambitions of her ruler meant nothing to Burgundy?

Innumerable examples might be cited to further illustrate the point, but a few will suffice. The "Glorious Revolution" of 1688 in England would probably never have taken place had James II been a less zealous and stubborn man: less zealous for Catholicism and less stubborn in his refusal to heed the anti-Catholic feeling of the majority of his subjects. How different the history of Europe might have been had the Turkish Sultan Suleiman the Magnificent, 1520-1566, been succeeded by a man like himself. Able, energetic, and ambitious, Suleiman once sent his armies to the gates of Vienna. Throughout his long lifetime the possibility of a Turkish conquest of Europe was ever present. But Suleiman's successor was a drunkard and a weakling, and Europe gained an invaluable respite. How different history would have been had Mohammed never lived! Mohammed developed a new religion and converted to it the obscure scattered tribes of the Arabian peninsula. Religious enthusiasm welded these hitherto inconsequential nomads into a mighty historic force. Within a century they conquered an empire stretching from the Atlantic to India. Islam became one of the world's great religions. And Mohammed, be it noted, was the only Arab before the twentieth century who influenced the rest of the world to any important degree.

When all proper allowances have been made for the force of ideas and the pressure of circumstances, who can say that the major dictatorships of the twentieth century owed nothing to the personalities of the dictators? What would Nazism have been without Hitler's magnificent oratorical gifts, keen insight into the German national character, and remarkable talent for manipulating men? The leader of Italian Fascism, Benito Mussolini, cared little for ideas of any kind. He espoused and abandoned one movement after another until he at last found one that would carry him to power. Once in power he repeatedly revised the doctrinal content of Fascism. In the final analysis, Fascism amounted to whatever Mussolini chose to say it was at any particular time. Yet who would be so rash as to assert that Mussolini did not influence the course of twentieth century history? Nobody is more vigilant than communists to assert the unimportance of individuals and the paramountcy of impersonal considerations (in this case economics) as movers in history. Yet communist and non-communist historians alike ascribe much of the credit for the success of the Russian Revolution of November, 1917 to the personal abilities of Lenin.

It has been asserted that the course of American history and perhaps that of the whole world would have been changed had the American Senate consented to U.S. membership in the League of Nations in 1919. The Senate was willing to accept League membership, but subject to some minor reservations authored by Senator Henry Cabot Lodge and others. President Woodrow Wilson, however, hated Lodge venomously, refused to accept anything that Lodge had helped to formulate, and vetoed the membership-with-reservations. The Senate refused to consent to membership-without-reservations. Consequently the United States never joined the League. Some students of international affairs still think that had the United States been a member from the first the League of Nations might conceivably have developed into an international force strong enough to have prevented World War II.

Oftentimes the course of great intellectual controversies is determined less by the intrinsic merits of the two cases than by the accident that most of the personal ability happens to be on one side. Such was the case in the dispute between the Jesuits and Jansenists in seventeenth century France. The issues need not concern us here, but the Jansenists were fortunate to have in their ranks Blaise Pascal, one of the authentic geniuses of his age and a master of French prose. The Jesuit order contained no one of comparable ability. An unequal literary warfare ensued. Its main result was that Pascal's scathing indictment of the Jesuits in his *Provincial Letters* struck a blow at the religious order from which it has never entirely recovered. Another aspect of French Catholic Church history illustrates the same point. The Church in the seventeenth century produced several men, Bossuet, Fenelon, and the aforementioned Pascal, who were at least the intellectual equals of any of their contemporaries. The nineteenth century produced more such figures of outstanding ability: Lammenais, Lacordaire, Montalembert, Dupanloup. But the intellectual challenge to French

Catholicism came primarily in the eighteenth century from the philosophes: Voltaire, Diderot, D'Alembert, Montesquieu, Rousseau, and others. In *that* century the Catholic side produced nobody of comparable intellectual stature. Not surprisingly, the ideas of the philosophes, generally inimical to organized religion, carried the day among most Frenchmen of intellectual pretensions.

History is replete with instances where imposing political or diplomatic systems crumbled when their creators passed from the scene. The empire of Alexander the Great had vanished entirely ten years after his death. The political and military skill and personal prestige of Charlemagne enabled him to rule most of western Europe for nearly half a century. Under his weak son and quarrelsome grandsons the Carolingian Empire was divided, and seventy-five years after Charlemagne's death it had ceased to exist. In eleventh century England William the Conqueror established what was for that time a centralized, efficiently managed state in which the nobles were clearly subordinate to the Crown. Some of his successors were weak men, however, and by 1215 the nobles had gained so much power that they were able to force King John to formally guarantee them a variety of rights and privileges in Magna Carta. The assassination of Wallenstein in 1634 destroyed any chance that the Catholic forces might win a general victory in the Thirty Years War for nobody else in Europe possessed at once the reputation, prestige, wealth, and military skill to raise and manage armies like those commanded by Wallenstein. The collapse of Bismarck's alliance system has already been discussed in detail.[1]

It is often alleged that certain developments are inevitable. In the long run this must frequently be true, but in the short run what happens depends to a large degree on what key individuals do. In our own time the mass passion of nationalism seems truly irresistible. It has already dissolved several empires and is currently in the process of liquidating others. Within the last century Great Britain has loosened the bonds that once held her empire together. Today such nations as Canada, Australia, India, and South Africa are still technically parts of what is called the British Commonwealth, but in practice they are as independent as France and Brazil. No doubt the United States would by now have gained a similar degree of independence had the American Revolution never been fought. If one considers, however, not these perhaps "in-

---

1. Cf. pp. 24-25.

evitable" triumphs of nationalism but one specific case, the actual American Revolution of 1775-1783, things do not look nearly so "inevitable." In fact, it is hard to see how the Colonies could possibly have won that conflict without George Washington and French aid. That the French Government eventually gave aid to the Colonies was due chiefly to the diplomatic talents of one man, Benjamin Franklin, and the activities of another, Beaumarchais. Franklin proved to be an extraordinarily shrewd envoy in Paris and Beaumarchais, who had been aiding the Colonies on his own for several years, succeeded in gradually drawing the French Government after him.

To turn to another country, it is quite possible, even probable, that England would have become a largely Protestant nation at *some* time, but she took the first steps towards becoming one at a *particular* time because of Henry VIII's infatuation with Anne Boleyn.

If Just One Thing Had Been Different . . . — Not infrequently great events are strongly affected by chance, accident, or the caprice of an individual. Some historians think that the whole course of the French Revolution, as well as France's subsequent political history, might have been altered substantially had Mirabeau lived longer. His death in 1791 deprived Louis XVI of his only able adviser and ended any real chance that the king might be able to control the Revolution and moderate it. Had Mirabeau lived it is not unlikely, though of course nobody can prove what might have happened one way or the other, that France would have developed a constitutional monarchy similar to that of England, the Reign of Terror would never have occurred, and Napoleon would never have come to power. Napoleon himself narrowly escaped death at the battle of Marengo in 1800, and some years earlier, during the Reign of Terror, he had once been slated for execution. How different might have been the history of Europe had be been guillotined with Robespierre in 1794! Indeed, it is one of the fascinations of history that no one can ever have any idea how much of it has been forestalled by the executioner. For generations Turkish sultans systematically massacred their male relatives to prevent palace intrigues against themselves, and punished unsuccessful generals and incompetent officials by execution. How much the general course of Turkish history might have been changed had some of these men lived is, of course, only guesswork, but it certainly would have been altered in many particulars. Who knows how many, if any, potential Einsteins, Freuds, and Lincolns perished in the murder factories of Nazi Germany or have been numbered among the millions "liquidated" by communist states in our own grim century?

It is likely, though impossible to prove beyond question, that the vanity of one man, Benito Mussolini, fundamentally altered the outcome of World War II. By autumn of 1940 Mussolini felt that his military accomplishments were embarrassingly less gaudy than those of his Axis partner, Adolf Hitler. In an effort to add to his prestige he invaded Greece. Winter came soon, the Greeks fought fiercely, and the spring of 1941 found the Italian armies still bogged down in the Balkan mountains. Partly to rescue his ally from this predicament Hitler overran the Balkan peninsula in the spring of 1941. These campaigns delayed the German invasion of Russia until June 22, whereas it had originally been scheduled to begin May 15. Given an additional five weeks of good weather it is probable that the German armies would have conquered all of Russia west of the Ural mountains. Had this taken place about the worst that Germany could have gotten out of the war would have been a negotiated peace that would have left her the undisputed master of the whole European continent.

It has been contended that the early death of Prince Felix von Schwarzenberg in 1852 altered the whole course of modern history. Schwarzenberg, the Chief Minister of the Emperor Franz Josef of Austria-Hungary, was the only statesman produced in that realm after 1850 whose abilities were comparable to those of the Prussian Chancellor, Bismarck. Had Schwarzenberg not died in early middle age it is possible that the German states might have been unified around Austria rather than Prussia. Now the Austrians and South Germans have been generally less warlike than the Prussians. Had the German Empire been centered around Vienna rather than Berlin perhaps the twentieth century would have been spared two world wars and their still incalculable consequences. All this is "history as if . . .," of course, but the point ought to be clear that the qualities of individual men, indeed the mere presence or absence of outstanding men, often makes a great difference in the turn taken by events.

Things Do Not Happen "In General"—One must never forget that no matter what abstractions and generalizations are used in historical description it is, after all, individual human beings who think and act and to whom things happen. One reads in a newspaper that "a mob" attacked a certain foreign embassy and were dispersed by the police with eight killed and twenty-seven injured. That "mob" was not just an abstraction. Its members were individual flesh-and-blood human beings like ourselves. They individually picked up cobble stones and threw them through the windows of the embassy. When the rioters were dispersed it was not "the mob" that suffered death and injury: it was eight separate individual persons who stopped bullets and lay dead on the pavement. It was no "mob," but twenty-seven other individuals, who got their heads cracked, or arms broken, or faces slashed and who ran off to nurse their wounds and their grievances. So it is with war, or government, or science, or literature, or anything else. "English literature" is not the product of "the English" in general: it is the sum of the writings of a number of individual Englishmen. "Science" does not produce anything. It is individual men working in laboratories who discover and develop all sorts of things. So with history too. Such general terms as "feudalism," "Reformation," and "Romantic Age" may be appropriately applied to certain periods or situations in history but one must remember that the generalization still refers to the deeds of innumerable individual men and women.

It is particularly important that people in a democracy not forget this elementary fact. Any society that prizes individual liberty and allows each man to take part in choosing his own government necessarily assumes that that man is free and that his individuality is meaningful and deserving of protection. While a society organized on collectivist principles of either the old peasant-village type or the modern totalitarian type may logically deny the importance of the individual man in history, it is surely absurd to be an advocate of republican government and at the same time a disciple of some determinist theory of history which envisions men as mere puppets manipulated by vast impersonal, irresistible forces.

Limitations on Individual Achievement—Yet if man is basically the master of his destiny he is never entirely so. No man, however talented and ambitious, can make the world over as he chooses. He can sometimes guide a people, change some of their ideas, make some of their ideas his own, and channel their desires and ambitions to suit his own purposes, but he can never for long force a whole people to do what is against their will. What any man can do is always limited in varing degrees by the physical environment, the level of literacy and political sophistication of his followers, the contemporary level of technological development, and other factors beyond his control. In a nation like the United States no President, regardless of his ability, can do just as he pleases. He is limited by the Constitution, the Supreme Court, Congress, and the regular governmental bureaucracy. These entities all have a constitutional position, enjoy public respect, have much direct power and indirect influence, and to a considerable degree run the government on a day-to-day basis in much the same way no matter who is President. Only in the most extraordinary circumstances could the President appeal successfully to the Armed Forces to allow him to override these other entities. There is no doubt that the United States Government operates more effectively when an able man like Theodore Roosevelt or Woodrow Wilson is President than it does under a Grant or a Harding. All modern governments in Western countries, however, are so complex and highly organized that they operate with moderate efficiency, at least for a time, no matter who is President or Premier. On a day-to-day basis they come close to running themselves.

Because political and social organization is far more complex than in times past the presence or absence of any one individual in an organization is less vital than it used to be. One has to turn back no further than the seventeenth century for examples. The assassination of Henry IV of France in 1610 plunged the French Government into fifteen years of chaos from which it emerged only when another strong man, Richelieu, came to power. By contrast, the late nineteenth century assassinations of Presidents Garfield and McKinley in the United States, President Carnot in France, and the Czar Alexander II in Russia, did not produce changes of equivalent importance in those countries. Doubtless we should be grateful, at least on humanitarian grounds, that the increasing complexity of human affairs is causing assassination to become a steadily less potent political weapon.

Do Times Make the Man? — Yes they do — sometimes. Men often gain a place in history because they happen to live in a particular time or place that offers them opportunities normally lacking. Undoubtedly many of history's great soldiers and statesmen would have made little impression on their times had not wars occurred and given them a chance to shine. William Pitt the Elder would be remembered only by students of the eighteenth century, and then only as an unimportant English politician, had not the Seven Years War given him a chance to become Prime Minister and display the abilities that led the Anglo-Prussian alliance to victory. Had not World War I thrust him into prominence Georges Clemenceau would have gone down in history as just another French politician and journalist, remembered chiefly for his mastery of caustic sarcasm. Winston Churchill is commonly regarded as one of the great men of the twentieth century yet, almost certainly, he would never have become Prime Minister of England had not World War II broken out. In the 1930's most Englishmen thought of Churchill as a brilliant political adventurer but so sadly deficient in judgment and stability that he would never gain high office. Most foreigners did not think of him at all. The outbreak of the war, however, discredited the "appeasement" policy of the existing English Government, Churchill got his chance, and the rest is well known.

A man born out of his time gets nowhere. There is no possibility that Charles XII of Sweden could repeat now his conquests of 250 years ago because Sweden is a small country ludicrously unequal to waging war for twenty years against modern Russia, Germany, and Poland combined. Even before the advent of atomic weapons the planes and tanks of these adversaries would have reduced twentieth century Sweden in a few weeks at most. It would have made no difference if the Swedish army had been led by Ghengis Khan, Julius Caesar, Hannibal, and Alexander the Great rolled into one.

In past centuries when most men thought of monarchy as the natural, normal form of government a political philosopher who defended the theory of the Divine Right of Kings was regarded as a sound, sensible man. But the greatest genius who ever drew breath would be laughed at and regarded with wonder if he advocated this conception now. The twentieth century simply no longer takes kings seriously. In the few countries where they still exist their function is chiefly decorative.

Sometimes a man is born at very nearly the right time, but not at exactly the right time, and so his ambitions remain unfulfilled. Such a one was the seventeenth century English Lord Protector, Oliver Cromwell. By the 1650's Cromwell had won the English Civil War, executed the Stuart King Charles I, and established himself as the dominant figure in the country. One of his ambitions was to form a coalition of the Protestant countries in Europe and to lead them in a "crusade" to extirpate Catholicism. Now Cromwell was a man of outstanding capacity and daring. Thirty years earlier, or thirty years later, his program would have had some chance of success. It would have gained at least the respectful attention of all the Protestant states and almost certainly the support of some of them. The 1650's, however, were precisely the wrong time for such a proposal. 1648 had seen the end of the Thirty Years War, a horrible conflict, partly religious and partly political, which had convulsed all western and central Europe for a generation. Much of the Germanies lay devastated, Denmark's armies had been soundly thrashed, Sweden was ruled by an eccentric woman with neither military interests or Protestant sympathies, and the Netherlands had just gained their independence from Spain after an eighty-year struggle. No important Protestant state in Europe had the slightest interest in starting a new religious war. All preferred to lick their wounds in peace. About 1620 Cromwell's design would have had far greater appeal for at that time the armies of the Catholic Emperor Ferdinand II were driving Protestants out of Bohemia and the legions of Catholic Spain were defeating the Protestant Dutch. Moreover, the two strongest Protestant states of the North, Denmark and Sweden, had good armies, that of Sweden being led by the brilliant, warlike king, Gustavus Adolphus. Cromwell's program would have had a chance to gain support about 1685 too. In that year Louis XIV of France revoked the Edict of Nantes, which had granted religious toleration to his Protestant subjects. Thousands of French Protestants (Huguenots) fled to other European countries. Everywhere they stirred up public sentiment against the monarch who had driven them into exile — and Louis XIV, it should be noted, was already thoroughly feared and hated by most of Europe because of his persistent aggressions against neighboring countries. In the same year, 1685, James II, a Catholic, ascended the throne of England, an event that caused widespread foreboding among his Protestant subjects. Unluckily for Cromwell's "Protestant Crusade" idea, however, the Lord Protector lived at the wrong time; a generation too late to have participated in the religious phase of the Thirty Years War, a generation too early to have perhaps started another such war. It has been well said that "History is made rapidly when a great man and his opportunity appear simultaneously."

The Man Who Is "Made" By a Movement—What history calls a "great" man is sometimes merely a sensitive, alert man. Not infrequently an individual is raised to power and prominence because he has a keen sense of what people want and what contemporary ideas and movements have a future. He vigorously espouses these and in due course becomes the "leader" of a movement. This is a common phenomenon in revolutions. In a revolutionary era there is much chaos and general bewilderment as established institutions break down or are attacked. All sorts of immoderate expectations are aroused by the slogans and shouts of the revolutionaries. A man of ability and daring who can discern what a large number of people want, and then espouse it vigorously, stands a good chance of emerging from the turmoil in control of a nation.

The classic example is the Russian revolutions of 1917. In March of that year the Czarist regime of Nicholas II collapsed and was replaced by a democratic government of the Western type, headed by Alexander Kerensky. Kerensky tried to keep Russia in World War I on the side of the Allies but the Russian people were thoroughly sick of the defeats, heavy casualties, corruption, and inefficiency that had characterized every aspect of the Russian war effort since 1914. Furthermore, the peasants were anxious to seize the lands of the aristocracy. In this situation Lenin, the prescient leader of the tiny Bolshevik movement, called for "Peace, Bread, and Land" — precisely what tens of millions of Russians wanted to hear. By November the Bolsheviks were able to overthrow Kerensky, and with surprisingly little difficulty.

Limitations Imposed by Impersonal Factors—If genius is to be effective a certain minimum level of general civilization is a prerequisite. No Abraham Lincoln ever appeared among the Australian Bushmen, no Galileo among the Iroquois, no Mozart among the Eskimos. The ideals and temper of a people likewise limit what any man can do or become among them. It is safe to say that the pacific Quakers will never produce a Ghengis Khan. Had ancient Sparta survived a thousand years its society would never have known a gentle apostle of peace like Tolstoy or Gandhi. An irreverent skeptic like Voltaire is inconceivable in the theocratic society of Tibet.

Uncontrollable Forces—Sometimes men set in motion forces which acquire a momentum of their own and largely pass out of human control, sweeping their instigators with them. Such was the famous case of the "war produced by railroad timetables" in 1914. The German General Staff possessed extremely elaborate plans for the movement of men and materials in the event of a European war against any opponent or combination of opponents. The French and Russian General Staffs had similar plans. Once Russia and France became allies in 1893 Germany was faced with the probability of having to fight both of them simultaneously in the event of war with either. In 1914 both France and Germany were relatively small countries with extensive road and railroad systems and efficient military and civilian bureaucracies. Each could mobilize an army, move men and supplies to the border of the other, and be ready for war within a few days. Russia, by contrast, was far larger, had fewer railroads and highways, and generally ran its public affairs much less efficiently than its western neighbors. Russian mobilization was expected to require about six weeks. In these circumstances German military plans called for hurling the bulk of the German army against France in the first days of a war and maintaining only a small holding force against Russia in the east. It was hoped that France could be defeated within six weeks, after which the whole German army could be shifted to the east to deal with the slow-moving Russians. In any political crisis where war was a distinct possibility the German government felt that it had to know very soon whether or not war was coming. If negotiations went on for weeks and then collapsed Russia would have had time to mobilize and Germany would be forced to fight two major opponents at once — when both were ready. Russia, on the other hand, precisely *because* her mobilization was so much slower than that of the other major Powers, would be anxious to begin it as early as possible whenever war threatened so as to minimize her initial disadvantage. Thus on July 29, 1914 when Russia began to mobilize in an effort to pressure Germany's ally, Austria-Hungary, to call off a war against Serbia, the German Government demanded that Russian mobilization cease within twelve hours. The Russian government refused. At once Germany declared war against Russia and invaded France. Germany was so fearful of losing her one priceless advantage over the Russians, time, and Russia was so fearful that her disadvantage might be made worse, that the mobilization of one set off a chain reaction that Heads of State seemed powerless to control. World War I was the result.

Summary—On the question of whether men control events or are controlled by them, Machiavelli probably came as close to the truth 450 years ago as anyone has ever done. He likened the course of events to a river: ordinarily controllable by building dikes and levees, but sometimes producing irresistible floods which sweep away the most careful designs of men.

A good specific example of the importance of one man in a historical epoch, and at the same time of the degree to which any man is dependent on circumstances, is the career of Napoleon Bonaparte. Between 1797 and 1812 his armies marched over Europe from Lisbon to Moscow. It is hard to imagine these sweeping French conquests without Napoleon. In particular, his invasions of Spain in 1808 and Russia in 1812, which led directly to his downfall, were dictated not by French national interests but almost entirely by his personal vanity and megalomania. For all his egotism, however, Napoleon was everywhere recognized as incontestably the ablest soldier of his age, indeed as one of the greatest of all ages. Significantly, Bernadotte who had once been one of Napoleon's marshals, and who became King of Sweden, advised the members of the anti-Napoleonic coalition to concentrate their efforts on the battlefield against those portions of the French army commanded by subordinates, and to attempt only a holding action where Napoleon commanded in person.

Yet it is quite evident that Napoleon's tremendous victories would have been impossible without a variety of political and technological innovations in the preceding fifty years which had made the French army, man for man and unit for unit, the best in Europe regardless of who commanded it. Between 1750 and 1789 the introduction of the divisional system had given France a more efficient mode of military organization than was possessed by her opponents. The quality of the artillery had been improved remarkably; schools for the training of officers had been founded; military mapwork had become much better; and thousands of miles of hard surfaced roads, which facilitated troop movements, had been built. The French Revolution of 1789-1797 had seen, simultaneously, the introduction of universal military conscription and the development of a fervent patriotic spirit among French soldiers. Neither had any counterpart in the professional armies of other nations. Between 1792 and 1797 these revolutionary armies won a series of impressive victories under a variety of generals. Thus Napoleon inherited an army superior in every respect to the forces of his opponents: huge in numbers, composed of better human material than old-style mercenary forces, filled with revolutionary enthusiasm, possessing a tradition of victory, and better organized and equipped than any contemporary force. When Napoleon's incomparable leadership was added the combination proved irresistible for fifteen years. But neither the man alone nor the instrument alone would have been sufficient. Both were essential.

CHAPTER VI

THE ROLE OF IDEAS IN HISTORY

Popular Ideas Determine the Character of Society—It has been said that ideas rule the world. Like most such blanket generalizations, the statement is exaggerated, but it does contain a large measure of truth for ideas are the cement that holds society together. If most men did not share the same fundamental concepts about how life should be lived and people should deal with one another society would have no stability. Suppose half the population of a given country believe firmly that war is the noblest expression of the human spirit, and the other half hold that war is never permissible; half that every respectable person should work for a living, and the other half that it is only more sensible to try to live by one's wits than by working; half that the fullest democracy is the only tolerable form of government, and the other half that absolute monarchy is the only acceptable form. The society in question would be torn to pieces by constant ideological battling. Community life is possible only because most people in civilized countries think theft and murder wrong, prefer to live in family units rather than in some other fashion, and do not ordinarily try to impose their own views on others by force.

Men always have ideas about how the world's affairs should be handled, and they always have ideals they wish to serve or see realized. Such will be the case as long as they continue to be men. Human beings have always had strong opinions about the relationship of man to God, of man to man, of God to government, of man to government, of freedom and order, of what is desirable and undesirable conduct, of what is bad but can be tolerated, of what is so bad that it cannot be tolerated, of how one should get along with neighboring peoples and nations, of how one social class ought to be related to another, and so on. The views on these matters that prevail at any one time and place powerfully affect the character of the society in question. A state like ancient Sparta, divided into two sharply distinct classes, rulers and ruled, and saturated with a spirit of militarism, is bound to be quite different in popular outlook than say, modern Denmark or the Netherlands.

Historians themselves unconsciously testify to the power of ideas as movers in history when they write their books in terms of ideas. The pages of textbooks are peppered with words like Romanticism, Enlightenment, capitalism, socialism, nationalism, Mercantilism, absolutism, Progressive Era, and others. Historian and reader alike take it for granted that such abstract designations are an accurate and meaningful way of discussing the past. In fact history touches the domain of ideas in more places than any other study, for history deals in some fashion with everything. New ideas in any field necessarily affect it.

The Pursuit of Ideals—The course of history has been changed in innumerable ways by the pursuit of ideals; perhaps most of all by the desire to secure universal acceptance for particular ideals. According to one theory about Alexander the Great, he was a genius who deliberately set out to spread Greek civilization to the then known world. Whether or not this was his intention, the effect was achieved anyway.

Christianity has always claimed to be a religion for all men. For 2000 years it has kept missionaries among non-Christians in an effort to convert them. In the nineteenth and twentieth centuries Christian ideas, Western dress, Western education, and improvements in sanitation, brought to Asiatics and Africans by missionaries, have begun to transform the lives of hundreds of millions of peoples. How many and how fundamental must have been comparable changes in the thoughts and habits of the innumerable millions of diverse peoples in the past to whom missionaries have gone!

Islam is a great fighting faith that has inspired scores of millions in the past thirteen centuries. Throughout the Middle Ages and early modern times the Islamic states of North Africa and western Asia posed a permanent threat to Europe. The Crusades, perhaps the most flamboyant episode of the Middle Ages, though complicated by many mean and petty motives, were at bottom a war of Cross versus Crescent, a struggle between rival universalist ideals.

The French revolutionaries of the 1790's were zealous to spread the gospel of Liberty, Equality and Fraternity to all mankind. The Revolutionary and Napoleonic armies scattered these ideas all over Europe and produced a ferment in the minds of men that destroyed monarchy in most of Europe in the succeeding century.

Woodrow Wilson's proclamations that the world should be reorganized on the basis of independence and democratic government for every nationality helped the Allies win World War I.

More important, perhaps, it also poured fuel on the fires of nationalist zeal in every corner of the globe.

No one in the mid-twentieth century needs to be reminded how strongly every part of the world has been affected by the communist ideal: to destroy capitalism and communize the earth. Pursuit of this objective has already entailed history's most sweeping governmental, economic, and social changes in half of Europe and Asia. It has produced several small wars and skirmishes, military preparations of unparalleled proportions and expense in the non-communist part of the world, and a permanent state of international tension as severe as any in recorded history.

No modern idea has affected history more than the passion of nationalism. In the nineteenth century it produced wars that unified Italy and Germany, and it stimulated rebellions in Poland, Hungary, Belgium, and half a dozen Balkan states. In the twentieth century its fruits may be seen on every side. Among them are claims that the Russians invented everything, denunciations of "Yankee imperialism," proud talk about "the African personality," claims for the pre-eminent virtue of something called "the American way," and milling faceless mobs bawling "Heil Hitler," "Il Duce," "Nasser," "Tito," "Kassem," or "Viva Castro." There is not an important part of the globe in which the ideal of nationalism has not produced "patriotic" political parties, wars of liberation, agitation for independence, governmental repression, and attempts to "re-educate" national minority groups in order to make them 100% patriots. It has been truly said that nationalism is the religion of the twentieth century.

One Man's Ideals—More narrowly still, the ideas of particular persons have markedly changed history. Such cases as Christ and Mohammed are obvious. In more recent times history has been heavily influenced by the writings of many men of much less than universal personal fame. Three examples, chosen at random, will illustrate the point. The nineteenth-century German historian Treitschke wrote a number of works suffused with a strident, aggressive patriotism. He laid heavy emphasis on the importance of national unity and strong centralized government. He is often credited with changing the attitude of the German people towards themselves: even charged thereby with being the indirect cause of the First World War.

In the 1890's there appeared a series of books by Admiral Alfred Mahan stressing the vital role of sea power in war and the achievement of national greatness. These works profoundly influenced many persons in military, naval, and governmental circles in a dozen major nations. The extensive naval building programs undertaken around 1900 by most of the Great Powers, and especially by Germany, were due in considerable measure to Mahan's books. The ensuing naval rivalry was one of the contributing factors to the First World War.

The conception of the American historian Frederick J. Turner that the whole course of U.S. history has been vitally influenced by the constant presence of the frontier has been much questioned on the ground of its intrinsic validity but there is no doubt whatever that it has markedly affected the way most Americans think about themselves and their history.

The Importance of Basic Attitudes—Oftentimes important historical changes are impossible without a prior or accompanying general change of mind or a new approach to a question. The momentous scientific advance of the sixteenth and seventeenth centuries — the theory of a sun-centered universe, the discovery of the laws of gravitation, the development of logarithms, calculus, and the telescope — were due quite as much to a changed basic approach to knowledge as to new inventions or the acquisition of new information. Natural scientists came gradually to think about the universe less in qualitative and philosophical terms and more in quantitative, mathematical terms. This proclivity in turn produced an awareness of the need for far more accurate instruments to weigh, measure, and observe, and the need for more advanced mathematical techniques to deal with the facts so acquired. The invention of slide rules, microscopes, more accurate clocks, barometers, and the development of new branches of mathematics soon followed.[1] It is an excellent example of a common historical phenomenon: when a need comes to be generally felt it is not long before ways are devised to satisfy it.

The modern Welfare State could never have arrived without a fundamental change in popular ideas about the nature and causes of poverty. In the nineteenth century the prevailing view was that poverty was akin to sin; that it was due to sickness, stupidity, or laziness, usually the last. Whatever its cause, it was held to be the responsibility of the persons concerned. If individuals or churches

---

1. This point is discussed in detail in Herbert Butterfield's excellent introduction to the history of science, *The Origins of Modern Science.*

wished to give alms to the poor on a personal basis that was their own business, but there was no obligation to do so. Gradually, however, since the end of the nineteenth century most people have changed their minds about poverty. Now, rightly or wrongly, they commonly ascribe it to social forces beyond the control of the individual and hold that the state is responsible for its relief. A clear indication of the change of mind may be gained from a comparison of the actions taken by Presidents Cleveland and Franklin D. Roosevelt, both Democrats, in the depressions of 1893 and 1933 respectively. In the first case, Cleveland interpreted the duty of the Federal Government to be to balance the budget, put its own affairs in good order, and let private businesses and individuals get out of the slump in any way they could. Roosevelt combated the depression of the 1930's by a program of extensive public works, governmental aid to industry, and massive federal spending. In each case a majority of the public approved the action taken.

People in the United States who still hold to the former view of poverty and believe that governmental interference in individual and private business affairs should be sharply reduced are mostly elderly and dwindling in number. Politicians who hold these views no longer possess widespread national appeal. It would be difficult to imagine either major party nominating a Cleveland, McKinley, or Coolidge now, let alone getting him elected. The Republican Party in the United States has come in practice to accept most of the New Deal just as the Tory Party in England has come to tacitly accept most of the social welfare legislation enacted by the Labour Government of 1945-1951. In both cases there has been many a wry face but the more conservative parties have given way, nonetheless, because the programs of their opponents have been approved by most of the voters — and they must approve too if they expect to win elections.

Ideals versus Realities—Very often ideas gain currency less from their intrinsic merit than from the fact that they are seen as alternatives to imperfect present concepts and conditions. Whatever exists, especially if it has existed a long time, shows its defects to the world. Whatever is proposed as a replacement displays chiefly its theoretical virtues and advantages. Only when the replacement is put into practice do *its* defects become apparent. In the late eighteenth and early nineteenth centuries laissez faire ideas enjoyed great vogue among the educated because people tended to contrast the speculative virtues of laissez faire with the obvious defects of

Mercantilism.[1] For seventy-five years before 1917 Marxian socialists enjoyed the tremendous propaganda advantage of being able to contrast the theoretical glories of a communist society with the glaring defects of the capitalist world. Undoubtedly many people became converts to Marxism thereby and others became willing to at least adopt a wait-and-see attitude towards it. Since 1917 this unfair advantage no longer exists. Russia has now been a communist state for nearly two generations; China and several eastern European countries since shortly after World War II. Now the comparison is between capitalist practice and communist practice; not the theory of one and the practice of the other. Not surprisingly, communism makes fewer intellectual converts than it used to.

Ideas As Fads—There are what can only be called fashions in ideas, too, quite as much as in ladies' apparel. In the eighteenth century, if one wished to command intellectual respect he endeavored to demonstrate, above all, that his ideas were reasonable and logical. Human nature was held to be everywhere the same. Law, politics, and governments were thought of as exact sciences. It was assumed that something near perfection could be achieved in each by "reasoning" about them. Early in the nineteenth century there developed a marked reaction to this cast of mind. So far did the pendulum swing[2] that the period is still called the Age of Romanticism. Now one with intellectual pretensions affected an exaggerated sentimentality, emphasized the beauties of everything "natural," considered the problem of government from the standpoint of past traditions rather than pure "reason," and regarded the diversity of human races, types, and habits, as a delightful, wholesome thing instead of merely evidence that some people were less civilized and enlightened than others.

Similar shifts of opinion have taken place in the United States. In the 1930's, for example, it was intellectually fashionable in certain circles to speak scathingly of the "failure of capitalism" in the midst of a paralyzing depression. Some then expressed sympathy, by contrast, for the "great experiment" being undertaken in Russia and professed confidence that the more disagreeable features of communism would soon disappear. Since World War II, however, Russia has become an enemy and past communist infiltration of

---

1. Mercantilism involved a great deal of governmental regulation of economic activity. Advocates of "laissez faire" believed in complete "Free Enterprise."

2. Cf. p. 40.

some government departments and defense establishments has been widely publicized. Now any American public figure who would express even the mildest approval of communism would be regarded as an ignoramus at best and a traitor at worst.

Popular Moods—History is affected a good deal, too, by changes in what ought more properly to be called attitudes than ideas. Centuries ago toleration was almost universally regarded as a shameful thing. One tolerated sin or error because he lacked the moral stamina to defend or impose the truth. The action of Inquisitors pursuing heretics and of Reformation Christian sects persecuting each other was well understood by persecutors and victims alike. Rare was the person who spoke out for the toleration of opponents' views. In modern liberal, democratic countries, by contrast, there is a widespread willingness to allow people to hold whatever political, religious, economic, or social ideas they choose, provided that they do not interfere with the exercise of these same privileges by others. A tolerant spirit is regarded as evidence of an enlightened, humane character; the mark of a civilized man. The practical consequences of this change of popular sentiment are enormous. Now the desirable aspects of toleration are surely so obvious and well known as to require no elaboration but, unhappily, the *consequences* of toleration are *not always* desirable. For instance, in a society where toleration is held to be a virtue minority groups and minority views of whatever sort have a much better chance to thrive than in a society where nonconformity is answered by repression. Unquestionably in the great majority of cases the whole society benefits thereby: human happiness is increased, serious thought is stimulated, and a lively diversity prevails over dull conformity. It is an ominous fact, however, that injudicious toleration can be the prelude to suicide. Each of the three major totalitarian movements of the twentieth century, Italian Fascism, German Nazism, and Russian Communism, could have been crushed had the governments they overthrew taken ordinary police measures against them resolutely and in time. Once in power, these totalitarian movements, particularly Nazism and communism, specifically disavowed toleration and persecuted their opponents without mercy, even to the extent of slaughtering them by the millions. This grim development has faced modern democratic states with an exceeding perplexing practical question: just how much toleration ought to be, or can be, extended to totalitarian movements which avowedly intend to use such generosity to grow strong enough to one day destroy their gentler opponents?

Repression of Ideas—A much debated aspect of this question is whether or not ideas can be destroyed by force. It was long an article of faith among believers in democratic government that this could not be done, but twentieth century experience has raised doubts. It seems reasonably clear that force can sometimes destroy an idea if it is applied with sufficient ruthlessness. Half measures never do for their chief result is to attract attention to what the persecutors wish to destroy, to make martyrs, and thus ultimately to stimulate the growth of the unwanted idea. The occasionally savage but always sporadic persecution of the early Christians by Roman Emperors is conceded by all historians to have stimulated rather than discouraged the growth of Christianity. The measures which the French Government adopted to combat its eighteenth century critics were sufficiently severe to cause the critics themselves a good deal of inconvenience, to make them feel persecuted, to gain them public sympathy, and to publicize their ideas, but not harsh enough to destroy them or even to seriously curb the dissemination of their ideas. Other regimes have been more thorough. The Albigensian heresy of the thirteenth century was destroyed by an alliance of the Inquisition and various French civil authorities. The Lollard heretics of the fifteenth century, followers of John Wyclif, were systematically repressed by the English Government and had virtually ceased to exist by 1500. In the sixteenth century Catholicism was practically extirpated in Scandinavia and Protestantism was never allowed to gain a foothold in Spain or Italy. The torture chambers and murder factories of Nazi Germany silenced all public opposition to the Hitlerite regime and exterminated most of its serious domestic opponents. The concentration camps of Communist Russia and China stifle all overt opposition in those states. The accompanying governmental censorship and propaganda monopoly exercised by these merciless dictatorships in time probably makes genuine a good deal of what was once purely formal support by their subjects.

Yet repression is never totally effective: and repression without any restraint whatever is never even attempted. Most people at times have sufficient humanitarian feeling, enough humility about the unlikeliness of their own infallibility, or sufficient sheer indifference, that they shrink from total repression. Sixteenth century

Catholics and Protestants were guilty of much mutual persecution but they always preferred to convert an adversary rather than take his life. Kings have not uniformly executed all their subjects who were suspected of republican sympathies. Modern totalitarian states approach the ultimate in soulless inhumanity more nearly than any past regimes but even the Nazis freqently preferred to work their victims to death over long periods instead of exterminating them outright. The communists often try to re-educate ("brainwash") ideological opponents instead of massacring them.

Ideas As a Facade—It is common knowledge that men and governments are prone to discover noble motives when explaining to the public why they propose to do something, when the real reasons are quite different and less attractive. (In fact, who is so saintly that he has not himself done this on occasion?) Neither persons nor governments, however, are ever completely cynical, nor, for the most part, do they wish to be. Even if governments sometimes pursue policies for quite earthy reasons (money, power, prestige, national vanity) they have to present those policies to their peoples in the shape of ideals. It is a tribute to the power that ideas exercise over men that public support cannot be secured otherwise. This is particularly obvious in the case of wars. How many Americans would willingly go to war and risk death if they were told that it was necessary to save the British Empire, or to enable J. P. Morgan and Company to make $500,000,000, or to enrich the munitions' manufacturers of half-a-dozen nations?[1] But if the war is represented as a struggle to make the world safe for democracy, or a war to make it possible to put an end to wars altogether, or a struggle to preserve the "American way of life" from destruction at the hands of Nazi Germany, international communism, or some other menace, public reaction is far different.

It used to be said, at least on the lower educational levels, that the American Civil War was fought over slavery. It was a useful corrective to this oversimplified view when books came increasingly to depict the war as a clash between the urban, industrial civilization and culture of the North and the rural, agrarian civilization of the South; and as a clash over states' rights. Even granting the latter, however, who can suppose that a war would ever have been fought over these latter issues alone? It was the slavery question,

---

1. These were not, of course, the real reasons for American entry into World War I. They are mentioned here because it was often alleged, for years afterward, that they were the decisive factors.

fanned into flame by the Abolitionists and *Uncle Tom's Cabin,* that caught men's minds, heated their imaginations, and outraged their moral sense.

Men Can Be Imprisoned by Ideas—Ironically, governments sometimes become the prisoners of the ideals they hold before their peoples. In the First World War Allied propaganda insisted that Germany was a vicious aggressor nation. She had started the war and her virtuous opponents were now fighting to make such action forever impossible in the future. Some, at least, of the Allied leaders knew that this was largely untrue but their peoples came to believe it thoroughly. The result was that at Versailles in 1919 Allied statesmen were powerfully pressured by public opinion to impose on defeated Germany a peace treaty more severe than some of them knew to be either just or wise. Peacemaking is bound to be difficult after any important modern war because governments systematically inflame the emotions of their peoples during the conflict in order to secure maximum support for the war effort. These emotions cannot be abruptly turned off once the war is over. If one is taught for three years that the Bulgarians are devils in human form, and that we Rumanians, along with our valiant allies, the Serbs, must fight to the last breath to avoid a fate worse than death at their hands, it becomes difficult to convince us, two years after the war is over and the diplomatic situation has changed, that the Bulgarians were really good fellows all along and that we ought to stand shoulder-to-shoulder with them to fend off the aggressions of the rascally Serbs. It is *possible* to do this, as is shown by the Allied reconciliation with Japan and Germany after 1945, in the face of the communist menace, but it is not easy.

This complication was rarer in the statecraft of the past. Centuries ago wars were usually the business of kings and governments rather than peoples. They were fought by professional armies or hired mercenaries, and it was not necessary to arouse public opinion at all. As a result, making peace and shifting alliances was much easier than now.

Idealism in Government—The previous examples have seemed to assume that governments are quite "hardheaded and practical," as current jargon has it, while their subjects are idealistic. This is not fair to governments, for politicians and statesmen are moved by ideals just as surely as their peoples, if not always in the same way or to the same degree. When a politician orates about the necessity of defending liberty against some menace or other he may very well be thinking primarily about some electoral advantage for himself or some financial gain for his friends, but in all likelihood he is just as interested as his listeners in defending liberty. If politicians did not stand in some measure for ideals that the masses desire they would not be elected. Even in totalitarian countries dictators cannot entirely ignore popular wishes and ideals. And no man, merely because he is elected to a public office, ceases thereby to care for the ideals that have meant something to him before. The reverse is nearer the truth. The politician is often elected to office *because* he is known or believed to be a strong supporter of some popular ideal. What reasonable man disbelieves that Woodrow Wilson sincerely thought that World War I was being fought to extend democracy and that the formation of a League of Nations would make it possible for men to abolish war altogether? Who can doubt that the government of Nazi Germany was not truly devoted to its despicable ideals when it kept tens of thousands of men occupied with the business, irrelevant to the German war effort, of exterminating millions of Jews, Poles, Yugoslavs, and other "racial inferiors"? Who can say that ideals meant little to the men who embarked upon the Crusades against the Turks, who have fought in the innumerable nationalist rebellions and wars of independence in the nineteenth and twentieth centuries, or who have devoted their lives to the effort to extend some brand of socialism to the world?

The day-to-day activities of governments of any sort are a blend of devotion to ideals and more or less cynical concern for power, prestige, money, and electoral advantage. A good example is the present government of Russia. It proclaims that its Marxist forefathers were responsible for bringing about the Russian revolution of 1917 which established the world's first communist state. This is largely false since the Czarist regime collapsed mostly from its own inefficiency and was succeeded by a liberal democratic government. It was this latter regime which the communists overthrew. Yet the communist contention is true in another sense for the Russian Bolsheviks had been agitating and planning for a revolution for decades, and when the opportunity at last arose they proved to be ready and able to seize power. Since 1917 the Russian Government has been true to communist principles in some respects. It proudly *asserts* that it is communist, tries to justify all its deeds by reference to Marxist theory, keeps an army of agents in every part of the world working for the spread of communism, and manages industry and agriculture largely through state rather than private processes. But it has done many empirical things too. Party members, industrial managers, scientists, and intellectuals in "classless" Russia enjoy many of the same special privileges and extra pay that their counterparts command in other countries. "Communist" Russia did not hesitate to ally first with Nazi Germany and later with "capitalist" England and the United States in World War II. The same wage differentials exist in Russian as in "capitalist" factories. Exceptions to the principle of collective agriculture are often allowed. All of these deviations from strict Marxist theory are laboriously "reconciled" with the dogmas of that "science" by the Party's experts on doctrine. The result is sometimes described as "enriching the storehouse of Marxism-Leninism." A careful examination of the words and deeds of other governments would yield similarly ambiguous results.

Prestige of Old Ideas—The course of history is influenced by the reverence men have for old, and frequently obsolete, ideas. Conservatives the world over commonly try to justify anything by demonstrating that it is derived from previous ideas, institutions, or usages. This process has been defined by a cynic as "the superstition that a thing is good because it is old, as distinguished from the opposite superstition that a thing is good because it is new." In totalitarian countries ideas can be imposed to some degree by force, but a commoner practice in free countries is to try to muster public support for some proposal by claiming that it resembles some generally praised concept from the nation's historic past. The proposal is said to be in accord with the ideas of the Founding Fathers, to be truly Christian, to represent sturdy British pluck, or to typify the finest traditions of Spanish chivalry.

Ideas Are Often Changed—Oftentimes a man's ideas are altered radically by his disciples and by succeeding generations. The process is simple. A man develops a certain idea on a particular subject or a new explanation of some important event. He expresses it with great clarity and verve. Soon it filters down to the population at large in a simplified, dogmatic form and becomes a cliche. This process is inevitable because a large sector of mankind is always too busy, indifferent, lazy, or mentally slow to take the trouble to try to understand anything complex. Thus our man's idea soon becomes a parrot cry on the lips of millions, uttered without thought on numberless occasions applicable and inapplicable. Who has not heard ad nauseam, "It takes all kinds to make the world"; "No more Munich agreements"; "You can't buy the friendship of foreign countries"; "Such-and-such a political party is for the little man"; and so on. Once these phrases had a specific meaning. Frequently there is still some truth left in them. After a time, though, they seldom have any specific or useful application to new situations. They become the banal battle cries of partisans who wish to spare themselves the painful chore of trying to think seriously about unfamiliar problems. George Washington's famous admonition to his countrymen to avoid entangling alliances had a specific and sensible meaning in his own day but in the mid-twentieth century world of nuclear weapons, intercontinental ballistic missiles, supersonic aircraft, and global ideological rivalry presents a totally different situation. Were Washington alive today it is safe to say that he would be far less enamored of his own axiom than are many of those who heedlessly invoke it. Frequently the "followers" of an ideal are considerably more zealous than its "creator." One can sometimes discuss the shortcomings of an idea in private conversation with the man who developed it, but seldom with one of his more fervent disciples. Many people dearly crave some ideal to believe in and devote themselves to, and when they get one they are reluctant to question it. How else does one explain the zeal of numerous advocates of Townsend Plans and Single Tax schemes, or of the followers of innumerable political and religious visionaries in all ages?

Many men would have higher reputations in written history if they were able to insist upon a certain meaning being given to their words and if they were able to control what later generations have chosen to regard as the true significance of their careers and writings. The eighteenth century French writer Jean Jacques Rousseau has been variously called a communist, anarchist, fascist, democrat, father of romanticism, and lunatic, by persons who have stressed some particular portion of his contradictory writings and ignored the rest. Charles Darwin applied his theory of the "survival of the fittest" only to biology. It was other men who extended it to sociology and politics. The nineteenth century visionary Friederich Nietzsche is usually regarded as one of the spiritual forerunners of Nazism. Had Nietzsche been alive in the 1930's, however, it is doubtful if he would have been happy in Hitler's Germany. He might well have been consigned to a concentration camp. Copernicus, Kepler, and Galileo had little notion of the revolutionary conclusions that subsequent generations would draw from their discoveries. Many of the leaders of the Protestant Reformation would be quite surprised could they come back to life and observe the theological ideas current in the churches they founded. The fourteenth century poet Petrarch thought the greatest work of his life, the one that would secure his place in history, to be a lengthy Latin poem, *Africa*. A number of sonnets which he composed in his native Tuscan dialect he considered to be of no importance. Ironically, in modern times the sonnets are widely read and admired while only Petrarch scholars venture to tackle *Africa*.

Ideas themselves often share the same fate as the reputations of their creators. When a defeated King John signed the Magna Carta in 1215, guaranteeing certain rights to "freemen," neither he nor the victorious barons had any idea that four centuries later another English king's subjects would successfully claim that "freemen" meant not barons only but every man born in England. The eighteenth century philosophes talked and wrote much about the equality of men, in theory — but the members of the Estates-General in 1789, though soaked in "philosophic" ideas, simply could not bring themselves to grant universal suffrage for that would mean surrendering political power into the hands of millions of illiterate French peasants. They resolved the dilemma by deciding that while everyone had equal rights one might not exercise his equality at the polls until he was properly trained and qualified, that is to say, until he had paid a sizeable sum in taxes. This nice distinction saved the sacred principle of equality and at the same time limited the suffrage to men of "substance and responsibility" (e.g., men of moderate wealth). Madame Roland, a prominent figure in the French Revolution, once remarked, "O Liberty, what crimes are committed in thy name." She might have said it just as appropriately about many other ideals as well.

Reaction Against Ideas—Ideas frequently exert a strong influence on affairs by the reactions they provoke. In the early nineteenth century a number of Englishmen, who are collectively termed The Manchester School, formulated a series of economic ideas in an effort to discredit the Mercantile System of economic thought prevalent in the eighteenth century. The keystone of the new system was laissez faire, that is the belief in the existence of an invisible law whereby the economic well-being of the whole society and of every person in it is, in the long run, best served by allowing all questions pertaining to trade, business, capital, and labor to be resolved without governmental interference. This view was regarded as veritable Holy Writ by most of the European and

American middle class throughout the nineteenth century even though it demonstrably kept industrial laborers in a position markedly inferior to that of their employers. Yet laissez faire policies were modified only slowly, in part because middle class people had struggled for generations to free themselves from the multifarious governmental regulations and burdensome taxes that had been such marked features of the old Mercantile System. Once freed from this web of bureaucratic restraint, it is understandable that their descendants could not imagine any possible good accruing from a return to the principle of state interference in commerce and industry.

It is a matter of common knowledge among professional politicians that great numbers of people do not vote *for* men or ideas but *against* them. Many persons will never vote for candidates with certain religious affiliations, regardless of their qualifications or party. What American has not known Democrats whose political conversation automatically begins with a denunciation of Herbert Hoover? How many millions must there be who will vote Republican to the day of their death because they despise Franklin D. Roosevelt and the New Deal? What tactic is commoner in American politics than to claim that one's opponent has socialist or communist sympathies, or that he is controlled by "Wall Street" or by other "interests" inimical to the welfare of all right-thinking people? A more amusing example, personally known to this writer, is that of an old lady who refuses to vote for any Democratic presidential candidate because only Republican Presidents have been assassinated!

Every free European country has many conservative people who vote automatically for what they regard as the most antisocialist candidate or party. Ever since 1789 French society has been divided between those who admire and those who hate French Revolutionary principles. Before 1945, at least, those who despised the principles generally tried to destroy democratic government in France without much regard for what might replace it. Those devoted to the Revolution seldom missed an opportunity to strike blows at the church, the army, and the aristocracy, the groups most firmly opposed to the principles of 1789.

Ideas As Myths—If enough people are moved by an idea, be the idea itself untrue, irrational, or nonsensical, it nonetheless acquires real historical importance. What people *think* is true is often more important in its influence upon the course of events than what is actually true. It is clear enough now that people of different religions can be loyal to the same political government, but sixteenth century men were convinced that it was impossible and so persecuted religious minority groups as actual or potential traitors. Napoleon Bonaparte, when Emperor of France, was a defender of order and property, but Napoleon, writing his memoirs on St. Helena, depicted himself as a son of the French Revolution, thereby creating a myth that helped his nephew to establish the Second French Empire a generation later.

While ideas which are really out-of-date often continue to exert an influence on many people once an idea is generally *recognized* to be out-of-date it becomes an object of derision and ceases to have any influence. A good example is the idea of "The White Man's Burden." In the late nineteenth century Cecil Rhodes, Kipling, and others were listened to with respect when they urged white men to assume the burden of raising up the colored races to civilized standards. In the mid-twentieth century, however, white men are less assured than they used to be of their "natural superiority" over the colored races. Most of them have ceased to believe that imperialism is either just or profitable. Hence if some present-day public figure seriously proposed the reconquest of Asia and Africa by Europeans on the ground that the natives of those continents would thereby be civilized he would get a cold reception. Some would regard him with amused tolerance as a relic of a departed age; others would denounce him as a heartless rascal or a would-be profiteer. There is hardly a surer way, now, to discredit a proposal of any sort than to claim that it is "imperialistic."

Rival Ideas—Quite often strongly held ideas clash. Sometimes one overcomes the other; sometimes they are compromised; sometimes one ultimately strengthens the other. In twentieth century America and western Europe there has been a protracted struggle between the laissez faire economic principles of the nineteenth century and the ideas of socialism. The result has been a draw: victory for neither one, but rather an amalgamation of the two. Private ownership and management have persisted from the laissez faire system, but subject to regulation, taxation, and vigilant scrutiny by governments.

A celebrated clash or irreconcilable ideas occurred in 1914. The international socialist movement at that time had long claimed that the true divisions in society were those of class, between capitalist and laborer. Laborers in one country were said to have nothing in common with capitalists of their own nationality but everything important in common with laborers of other countries. Wars arose because rival gangs of capitalists competed for markets. The outcome meant nothing to workers anywhere. In case of war the workers in every country should refuse to bear arms against their fellows elsewhere, for only the capitalists benefitted. When the First World War began, however, all the belligerent governments called upon their male subjects to perform their patriotic duty of defending the fatherland. Socialists were placed in a dilemma. Their nationalist feelings soon proved stronger than their socialist principles. With few exceptions German socialists went to the front to fight for Germany, French socialists to fight for France, and English socialists to fight for England. Socialist internationalism was put in cold storage for the duration. A similar instance occurred in England in the 1930's. The English Labour Party was officially committed to socialist principles and contained many pacifists who denounced all wars. With each advancing year, however, the aggressions of Hitler and Mussolini made it increasingly apparent that, unless resisted soon, the whole continent might be turned fascist — an ideology to which the Labour Party was adamantly opposed. The dilemma was resolved, as in 1914, by the abandonment of pacifism.[1]

Ideals do not necessarily destroy or weaken each other, however. Sometimes each of two different ideals strengthens the other. A good example is the historic relationship of Russia and Poland. For centuries Russia has sought to make Poland a province in the Russian Empire or, failing that, to control a nominally independent Poland. Just as persistently the Poles have resented and resisted Russian domination. Most Poles have always been Roman Catholic in religion and most Russians Orthodox. With the passage of time Polish nationalist dislike of Russian rule has been intensified by the religious difference between the two peoples. Polish nationalism and Polish attachment to Catholicism have thus each been strengthened by the other.

Dilution of Ideals—Ideals do not always win. Any struggle for an ideal almost invariably involves quite different ideals and "practical" considerations as well. In pursuit of the latter the original ideal is frequently forgotten. The Thirty Years War, 1618-1648, is a good example of a historic situation which combined clashing

---

1. Pacifism has been aptly defined as, "My enemy, right or wrong."

ideals, personal and national ambitions, and sheer greed for plunder. In its early stages the war was basically a contest of principles: that is to say, it was more about Catholicism versus Protestantism than about anything else. By the 1630's, however, this was no longer the case. Soon after the war began most of the Catholic states in Germany rallied to the support of the Catholic Emperor Ferdinand II. However, the sweeping military success of the Emperor's famous mercenary, Wallenstein, frightened the Catholic states nearly as much as it did Wallenstein's Protestant opponents. They feared that once all the Protestants were defeated Wallenstein might well turn on them and simply absorb them into his employer's Hapsburg Empire. Accordingly, the members of the Catholic League in 1630 put pressure on Ferdinand to dismiss Wallenstein — a clear case of local and dynastic interests taking precedence over religious ideals. Similar developments took place on the Protestant side. First, Lutheran Denmark entered the war on the side of the German Protestant states — for a variety of motives, only one of which was religious. The Danes were beaten, but then Lutheran Sweden sent an army headed by one of the great warriors of the age, King Gustavus Adolphus. The German Protestant states were nearly as frightened of their new Swedish allies as of their Catholic enemies, and for much the same reason that the Catholic states feared Wallenstein. Accordingly, they cooperated most reluctantly with the Swedes. On one occasion Gustavus secured the alliance of Brandenburg, one of the Protestant states he had come to Germany to "defend," only by overawing its capital with his artillery. The Danes, for centuries enemies of the Swedes, had difficulty hiding their hope that Gustavus would be driven out of Germany by the Imperial armies, religion or no. Meantime, Richelieu, a Cardinal in the Catholic Church and the virtual ruler of Catholic France, was heavily subsidizing the Protestant Swedes to fight the Catholic Emperor. His motives were entirely political. The rulers of France and the Hapsburgs had been rivals for over 150 years; and he wished to prevent the Hapsburgs from conquering all central Europe. Richelieu tried to save appearances by having Gustavus promise not to molest Catholics in lands conquered by the Swedes, a pledge which the King largely ignored. The last stages of the war were, in the west, mostly a dynastic conflict between Spain and France, both Catholic states; and in Germany mainly a series of wholesale marauding expeditions by the Swedes. Altogether, one would have to say that the Thirty Years War was fought fundamentally for an ideal, religion, in the sense that had it not been for the religious issue the war would probably never have occurred. Nonetheless, the ideal became so obscured and compromised by national fears and rivalries, by the personal ambitions of some of the participants, and by the threat that a sweeping Hapsburg victory would pose to the rest of the continent, that in the later stages of the war religion had been largely forgotten.

Thus ideals and principles possess great power to shape history, but they are constantly being altered, thwarted, or diluted by contrary ideals and by the activities of men and governments who have no principles beyond the acquisition of office, money, and power.

CHAPTER VII

How Organizations Influence History

The Nature and Proclivities of Organizations—We have seen that the influence of individuals in history is often specific and obvious; the influence of ideas equally clear, if less specific. History is also made by institutions. Indeed, written history is largely concerned not with pure ideas, not with personal biography, but with the doings of such collectivities as governments, churches, armies, officials, and organized social groups. Each claims to stand for some great cause or to perform some indispensable service. To a considerable extent this is true, but each is also swayed by immediate material interests often at variance with its theoretical pretensions.

Institutions and organizations are formed for many reasons. Some, such as armies and government bureaus, exist in every civilized society because without them society could not be effectively administered or defended. Some institutions arise because social forces; e.g., ideas, beliefs, attitudes; tend to find institutional expression. Others arise because it is usually difficult for one individual to achieve much without joining an existing organization or founding a new one to express and promote his ideas. Whatever its origin, an organization seeks to increase its numbers and activities, to extend its powers and influence, and to perpetuate itself. The officials of a long established institution like a church or a national army commonly regard themselves as the heirs of their predecessors and trustees for those who will succeed them. Consequently they seek to defend and protect their institutions, and usually to aggrandize them as well. This attitude has been exemplified many times in European history when secular governments have confiscated church lands. Quite apart from the justice or injustice of any particular confiscation, churchmen have invariably denounced such seizures because they feel that they themselves do not own the property in question. It belongs to their church as an entity. They are only entrusted with its care and are thus obligated to defend it, whatever might be their personal opinions about a particular confiscation.

People who belong to an organization or are employed by it thereby involve their lives, careers, and ambitions in its fate. Predictably, most of them do their best to add to its power and authority, either for the sake of this alone or because they think they can thereby better perform their own tasks, or for both reasons. Only a rare person will uncomplainingly subordinate his personal or organizational interest if he thinks it conflicts with a greater public interest. This is attested by the hordes of lobbyists for every sectional, class, racial, and economic interest who harass every legislative body in the world.

Governments—Governments have always exercised enormous influence in human affairs. It has been a common characteristic of governments in all times and places to try to control their subjects more effectively, to grow, to expand, and to try to dominate neighboring governments or peoples. Modern governments have at their disposal all the products of the Industrial Revolution and can thus pursue these natural tendencies more effectively than in the past. They register their subjects at birth, fingerprint them, issue them identification cards, teach them to be national patriots, induct them into armies, release them at their (the government's) pleasure, and tax them all their lives at rates and under conditions of the government's own choosing. All this influences history so heavily and so obviously that written history used to be chiefly the history of governments and their activities. It is still the core of any general history.

Churches—The influence of churches is nearly as extensive. In the Middle Ages it was perhaps even greater. How pallid and empty would be the history of Europe from the fifth to the fifteenth centuries if church history was left out of it. The church possessed a whole hierarchical organization of pope, cardinals, archbishops, bishops, canons, abbots, and priests. It was their concern to lead the whole society towards eternal salvation. The organization they served was regarded as the fountainhead of the moral and ethical ideals that were supposed to guide the whole society. The church possessed vast wealth, chiefly in the form of huge tracts of land, in every Christian country. It had its own administrative, legal, and tax system. All these cut across national boundaries. Its hold on the minds of the mass of men is impossible to determine precisely but it was surely immense. The church claimed that the things of Heaven took precedence over the things of this world. In practice this meant not only that Christian principles but also all its own possessions and privileges took precedence over the powers, interests, and ambitions of secular institutions. Real or apparent conflicts between men's allegiance to their civil and their ecclesiastical superiors were incessant. Battles between kings and churchmen over the boundaries of their jurisdictions went on for centuries. In general, medieval kings conceived the ideal church-state relationship to be one in which they were supported by a "loyal" church whose major dignitaries within their own dominions were appointed and controlled by themselves. Most churchmen saw it as an arrangement whereby "loyal" kings supported their principles and granted them numerous immunities and privileges, but otherwise left them alone. No theme pervades medieval history with greater persistence than the struggle of these two institutions, state and church, for domination over the other.

This whole elaborate ecclesiastical system still exists in the modern world, of course, and quarrels between churches and states have by no means vanished, yet the influence of churches is much diminished in Western society from what it was centuries ago. Modern governments more and more give mere lip service to Christian principles, and twentieth century Europe and America contain scores of millions of people who are not even formally affiliated with any church — a situation inconceivable in the Middle Ages.

Armies—The needs, deeds, and make-up of armies exert a variety of influences on any society that possesses military forces on a permanent basis. A sharp social cleavage between aristocrats and commoners has existed in all European countries until very recent times. There were many reasons for this, not the least of them being the persistence with which armies and navies drew officers from the nobility and ordinary troops from the ranks of the common people. Armies heavily influence a society economically too. To recruit, train, clothe, feed, pay, supply, transport, and pension hosts of soldiers costs vast sums of money, not to speak of the tremendous cost in modern times of weapons and weapons' research. The money has to be raised by governments. Whether they get it by borrowing or by levying additional taxes on their subjects the whole society is affected in innumerable ways, obvious and subtle. How can one overrate the importance of the Prussian army in the history of the eighteenth century Prussia when the government of that state devoted 90% of its budget to military expenditures in the 1750's? It would not be far from the truth to assert that the army *made* Prussia, for without a strong, efficient army the scattered conglomeration of north German states collectively called Prussia would never have been able to survive and grow into a great nation.

One of the reasons for the French Revolution was the bankruptcy of the government of Louis XVI. A few years before the revolution two-thirds of the government's budget was spent directly or indirectly on the armed forces. In most of the years since World War II American military expenditures have totaled something like two-thirds of the annual federal budget, a sum in the neighborhood of $40-50,000,000,000 a year. Some observers think that if these vast sums could be diverted to the production of consumer goods or spent for other peaceful purposes American life would be transformed. Others insist that it is the military expenditures themselves which keep the economy going: that if all American industrial production was channeled into civilian goods the market would soon be saturated and the country plunged into a paralyzing depression. Regardless of which judgment is correct, or if either is, the influence of the armed forces upon contemporary American life can hardly be underrated. The desires and interests of the military are generally given precedence over any others; they absorb two-thirds of the annual budget; they commandeer the best scientific brains in the land for military research; and they subject most of the younger male population to military service of one type or other.

Through the centuries current modes of military organization have strongly influenced the character of society as a whole. The pre-eminent position of the feudal nobility in medieval society was due in the first instance to their own military traditions and to the supremacy of cavalry in contemporary wars. The nobles were the only persons wealthy enough to possess horses. The decline in the importance of the aristocracy in the late Middle Ages was accelerated by changes in the composition and weapons of armies. The widespread use of mercenary troops and the introduction of weapons like pikes, longbows, and hand guns, that could be used effectively by foot troops of common birth against feudal cavalry, all diminished the importance of the aristocracy in war and therefore their importance in society as a whole.

It has been claimed by the German historian Werner Sombart that the rise of mass armies in the last two hundred years gave great stimulus to the Industrial Revolution. Mass armies need

hundreds of thousands of guns, swords, canteens, uniforms, bando-
leers, and other equipment — all exactly alike. According to
Sombart, these demands acted as a powerful stimulus to develop
machine mass production. He thinks further that the discipline
imposed on armies is similar to the sort required for efficient factory
production and that the latter was consciously modeled on the
former.

Armies sometimes virtually support a state rather than the
reverse. The case of Prussia has already been cited. An eighteenth
century figure once remarked that Prussia was not a state, but a
recruiting ground for the Prussian army. In any event, the Prussian military tradition has strongly affected all German society.
Down to 1945 military interests and considerations were consistently given precedence over civilian. Between 1871 and 1918 the
Imperial German Army was virtually an independent political
force. Its commanders were responsible not to the German parliament or even to the nation but to the Emperor personally. The
General Staff maintained its own diplomatic service independently
of the regular diplomatic corps. It was very nearly a state within
a state. It is hardly surprising that in World War I the leaders of
the army, Hindenburg and Ludendorff, assumed the direction of
political affairs too. After 1916 they ruled Germany as co-
dictators, in all but name.

Legislative Bodies—Parliaments also exert a powerful influence
upon the course of human affairs. From the thirteenth century the
English Parliament has been a partner with the Crown in the
governing of that country. In the sixteenth century, under the
Tudor dynasty, the Crown dominated Parliament, but in the seventeenth many of the landed aristocracy and the commercial classes,
the groups most heavily represented in Parliament, came to dislike
the political and religious policies of the Stuart kings. Eventually
their grievances became focused in the House of Commons whose
members, moreover, felt slighted personally by the kings. They
regarded the Commons as an august body of noble antecedents; a
full-fledged partner of the Crown; not a mere handmaiden to be
summoned to do the king's bidding and then to be dismissed.
Eventually the Commons became sufficiently distrustful of King
Charles I, and resentful of what they regarded as his high-handed
treatment of them, that they began the civil war of the 1640's.
The Parliamentary forces won the war, as well as a briefer and
bloodless later conflict in 1688. The consequences were momentous.

Parliament has been the dominant force in English political life ever since; and in the nineteenth and twentieth centuries parliaments, modeled on that of England, have been established in every part of the world.

Bureaucracies—In all organized societies the bulk of the day-to-day business of ruling is carried on by regular governmental departments, bureaus, and commissions, whose membership is permanent, professional, and largely unaffected by political changes in top governmental circles. In the last two centuries France has enjoyed, or at least experienced, a dozen different political regimes, most of them violently hostile to principles cherished by some of the others. Yet, whether France is governed by Louis XVI, Robespierre, the Directory, Napoleon I, Napoleon III, or any of a variety of republican regimes, her bureaucracy has remained little affected by these surface oscillations. French civil servants have grown steadily more numerous and powerful, and they rule France today in much the same fashion as did their ancestors in the eighteenth century. The reason is not difficult to find. Any government that steadily assumes more functions and responsibilities, as all modern governments do, needs more and more civil servants to carry out its orders and plans. There is always a great deal that civil servants can do unobtrusively to promote or speed up what they approve and to impede what they dislike. Professional civil servants stay at their posts year after year for decades while their political superiors are changed every few years, or even months. These superiors, consequently, have to depend heavily on the advice of the permanent bureaucrats in all cases and entirely in many. Thus government can be likened to an iceberg: nine-tenths lies beneath the surface, escapes close public scrutiny, and is much the same at all times.

Specific examples can be drawn from the history of many countries. The French administration at every level systematically ignored the doings of the Cabinets that rose and fell in Paris every few months under the Third and Fourth Republics, 1871-1958. The German Weimar Republic, 1919-1933, was weakened considerably by the fact that the permanent judiciary and civil service were predominantly monarchist in political sentiment and thus out of sympathy with most of the Republic's projects and even with its ideals. The English Labour Party complained for years that the permanent officials in the Foreign Office were nearly all Conservative in politics and outlook, and that it was thus impossible for a

Labour Government to ever effect meaningful changes in the spirit of British foreign policy. In the United States many of the bureaus created during the depression of the 1930's cling tenaciously to life years after the tasks for which they were created have been completed. Their members strive to preserve their jobs by finding new things to do and by devising new arguments to convince Congress of their importance and consequent need for appropriations.

Occupational Organizations—The eighteenth century philosophe Condorcet thought that this general tendency (above) was the source of many of the world's ills. In his view, organizations are originally founded to perform some useful service for the whole community. As time passes, however, their members try to establish monopolies over whole fields of knowledge or human activity. They become mere esoteric societies, devoted chiefly to exploiting their advantageous position for their own benefit and no longer serving any general public need. The history of the medieval guilds follows this pattern closely. Organized originally to insure a decent livelihood for the persons engaged in a certain craft or trade, to maintain standards of workmanship, and to insure a fair selling price to the public, they eventually became closed corporations whose members sought to exploit the public for their own profit. The masters of a guild restricted the number of apprentices to be trained and insisted upon working practices which had the general effect of insuring that there was always more work available than trained guild members to perform it. This allowed the guildsmen to dictate the conditions under which they worked. Many modern labor unions and organizations in the "learned professions" do much the same thing.

In the case of the labor unions they are usually founded by idealistic men who are laborers or craftsmen themselves. In their early years the union demands are commonly for higher wages, better working conditions, recognition by employers, and other objectives directly connected with the work and living standards of the members. In time, however, many of them come to be led by men who do no manual labor, and in some cases who have never done it, but who are professional "labor experts." These persons are sometimes less concerned with the real interests of the rank and file than with increasing their own power. They often feel that they must get "better" contracts for their unions every year in order to appear "successful" and thus to keep their own jobs and get raises for themselves.

In the case of certain occupations where a great deal of formal education is required in order to perform one's professional tasks the members often determine the conditions for admission to the profession and sometimes even control the facilities for training prospective new members. Thus it is easy for them to limit the numbers who enter the profession and thereby assure that their services will always be in demand and that they will be able to charge fees that nearly everyone else thinks much too high.

Political Organizations—Political life is profoundly affected by institutions of every sort and by the power of organization. Well organized and handsomely financed lobbyists deluge legislators with "facts," cajole them, promise them, and even threaten them with retribution in the next election, in the effort to persuade them to vote in accord with the desires of a certain group, institution, or interest. The outcome of elections in a democratic country such as the United States is as often due to efficient political organization as to the innate worth or attractiveness of a party's platform. All professional politicians know this, speak openly of it among themselves, and consistently act on it. To the ordinary professional politician "issues" are largely a nuisance. The important business is to get the party nominees elected, for that means power for the party and jobs for the party faithful. To win one must have appealing candidates, to be sure, and it usually helps to appeal to sectarian emotions and rancors of various kinds, but one also needs lots of money — for campaign propaganda, speakers, radio and television advertising, door-to-door political canvassers, and cars to take the aged, infirm, or lackadaisical supporters to the polls on election day. The party that does the most and the best in these respects frequently wins the election regardless of the comparative merits of the candidates or the party platforms.[1]

Institutions Inspire People—Institutions exert a strong influence on individuals too. Many a man supports an institution as zealously as an ideal, sometimes because he sees the ideal incarnated in the institution. The "company man" type is well known in any business organization. The modern labor movement owes much, perhaps most, of its success to the efforts of dedicated men who spent (and still spend) their lives struggling to improve the livelihood of their fellow workers. Every government agency has its

---

1. This does not mean, of course, that professional politicians are entirely devoid of ideals. Cf. Chapter Six, pp. 87-88.

quota of "tireless public servants" who are such in reality as well as in name. Every school system has a number of teachers, selfless and devoted, who genuinely give their lives to the education of the young. Every army contains some professional officers who are zealous patriots; who risk popularity and sometimes even their careers by their constant prodding efforts to keep their nation's defenses up to date. In World War II the loyalty of one such group, high-ranking German officers, was put to a sore test. Many of them were convinced that Hitler was leading Germany to ruin, yet only with difficulty could they bring themselves to plot against him. They were torn between loyalty to country and loyalty to their leader, the constitutional commander-in-chief to whom they had sworn an oath. The latter was reinforced by the consideration that to plot against the Head of State in wartime is bound to bear at least the appearance of treason. The makeshift nature and unsuccessful outcome of the various plots against Hitler was due chiefly to the inability of the plotters to resolve this dilemma in their own consciences.

Social reform organizations of all sorts — antislavery societies, temperance groups, charitable organizations, civic reform movements — always owe much to individuals who are inspired by their purposes and who serve them loyally for years.

The Prestige of Age—An institution, like a person, that has grown old, often enjoys a measure of prestige and influence for that reason alone. How often do businesses stress that they were "founded in 1844"! How many are the schools and other public corporations that emphasize that they were established 200 or 500 years ago! They know the respect that people accord to mere age and durability. Dictators know this too. A dictator is commonly a parvenu; one who has seized power through some coup d'etat; one who is without constitutional standing or roots deep in his nation's past. Often he will try to acquire some respectability by making friends with an ancient entity of some sort or linking himself to it. Thus in 1801 Napoleon ended the estrangement of the French Revolution from organized religion by concluding his famous concordat with the Vatican, the oldest monarchy in Europe and the center of the Church to which most of Napoleon's subjects belonged, at least nominally. In 1810 he took as his second wife a daughter of the Hapsburgs, one of the most ancient and prestige-encrusted dynasties in Europe. A more recent "Napoleonic type," Mussolini, gained the passive toleration, if not the active support, of the Papacy by his concordat of 1929 which ended a sixty-year feud between the Vatican and the Italian state.

Parvenus frequently try to secure the prestige of ancient traditions or institutions in cruder ways than this. They erect statues and memorials to past national heroes. They try to represent themselves as prototypes of these illustrious ancients or to identify themselves with glorious periods in the past — all in the hope that some of the gilt will rub off on themselves. Thus Napoleon spoke familiarly of Charlemagne as "my predecessor"; Louis Philippe, the "citizen king" of France, 1830-1848, made a great show of bringing Napoleon's corpse back from St. Helena for a ceremonious burial in Paris; and Mussolini persistently referred to his Italy as "the new Roman. Empire."

Altogether, the day-to-day course of events is undoubtedly determined more by the routine activities of institutions than it is by the deeds of exceptional individuals or the force of ideas. The student should always keep in mind, however, that distinctions of this sort are artificial. It is men who compose institutions, and the institutions themselves are often called into being in an effort to turn an idea into a reality.

CHAPTER VIII

ECONOMIC AND TECHNOLOGICAL FACTORS IN HISTORY

The economic interpretation of history is invariably associated with the name of Karl Marx. Marx held that the manner of production in economic life was much the most important factor in determining every aspect of human existence. At any stage in history those who controlled the means of production were thereby in a position to dominate society as a whole. If the means of production changed or fell into new hands all the other aspects of life changed rapidly too. History was chiefly the record of the efforts of the masses to make a living. This produced a constant class conflict between the "haves" and the "have nots," those who controlled the means of production and those who were forced to depend on them. Marx did not entirely rule out noneconomic factors, but many of his disciples did, perhaps because much of his own writing was rather vague. Many objections have been raised against the economic interpretation of history. The reader who has gotten this far will already be aware of some of them. Others will be pointed out later in this chapter. To demonstrate that history is not determined exclusively by economic considerations, however, does not diminish the fact that they do influence it heavily. Marx was guilty of exaggeration but his writings drew attention to the importance of factors long overlooked.

Class Rivalries—Class conflicts with some economic basis are common in history. In the Middle Ages serfs and feudal nobles stood at opposite poles in the economic order, the serfs performing the physical labor required to maintain the whole society and the nobles being the primary beneficiaries. The social cleavage between the two groups was a reflection of the economic difference. That the serfs were by no means always content with their lowly lot is evident from the frequency of peasant rebellions, especially in the later Middle Ages. One of the major basic causes of the French Revolution was the gaping gulf in French society between the privileged classes, nobles and clergy, who controlled much of the nation's wealth but were exempt from most taxes, and the bourgeoisie and peasants who did most of the work that supported the country but who were taxed heavily and disdained as a lower social order. In the last century the antagonism between the capitalist and laboring classes in most European countries has been constant and frequently sharp: sharpened, in fact, by the influence of Marxist ideas themselves.

Limitations Imposed by Economic Factors—Studies in economic history usually improve our understanding of particular periods and of the actions taken by contemporaries. Research into the economic life of ancient Rome has indicated clearly the extent to which unsolved economic problems contributed to the downfall of Antiquity's mightiest empire. Roman industry was not sufficiently developed to enable cities to be self-supporting. Instead, Roman cities were parasitic, constantly drawing in wealth from the countryside. For centuries after the Carthaginian Wars (third and second centuries B.C.) small independent farmers were driven off the land due to their inability to compete with huge plantations owned by aristocrats and worked by hordes of slaves taken in Rome's victorious wars. The formerly independent farmers gravitated to the empire's cities. A few were able to find employment in handicraft industries, but most became part of the ever growing useless urban mobs who had to be fed and kept amused to prevent them from becoming politically dangerous. The expense to the government was crushing, and the situation grew steadily worse with each passing generation. The currency was inflated and taxes were raised until the taxpayers grew apathetic or fled the soil, but the problem was never solved. More fundamentally still, Rome throve for centuries by conquering new lands and systematically looting them of stored wealth and slaves. Eventually there was nothing left to conquer and the empire was forced to live on its own resources and to bear the cost of administering and defending the conquered territories as well. The burden was crushing and Rome eventually collapsed beneath it.

Economic Motivation—More restricted studies have been equally enlightening. L. B. Namier's *The Structure of Politics at the Accession of George III* investigated the financial status of members of the English Parliament in the mid-eighteenth century and thereby contributed significantly to our understanding of the political history of the period. Charles A. Beard's *An Economic Interpretation of the Constitution* analyzed the economic circumstances and interests of the members of the U.S. Constitutional Convention, thereby making more intelligible their words and deeds at that gathering, as well as many of the features of the Constitution they created.

Ironically, recent studies of the Industrial Revolution have shown that the truth can sometimes be distorted by investigations into economic history. Most of the persons who were formerly attracted to this field of history were socialists. Their desire to discredit capitalism caused them to paint the squalor and social degradation of early nineteenth century industrial laborers in darker colors than the facts warranted.

Instances are common in which the course of political and even religious history has been strongly affected by economic considerations. The confiscation of monastic lands under Henry VIII, and their subsequent sale at bargain prices to English landowners and merchants, gave these powerful groups a vested interest in defending the religious changes introduced by Henry VIII. Some historians think it the most important single factor in the ultimate victory of Protestantism over Catholicism in England. All those who received confiscated church lands during the French Revolution thereby acquired an interest in the success of the Revolution. If the Revolution was crushed and the Bourbons returned they stood to lose their newly acquired properties. The establishment of a National Bank in 1791 at the instigation of Alexander Hamilton provided the United States with a currency that could be used in every state. The advantages to businessmen were obvious and their support for the newly formed government was thereby secured. A century earlier the foundation of the Bank of England stabilized English finances and made it easier for the English Government to finance its eighteenth century wars. One of the reasons the Industrial Revolution began earlier in England than on the Continent of Europe was the greater order existing in English finances and the comparative ease with which money could be borrowed to invest in industrial enterprises. The success of the Communist Revolution in Russia in 1917 was due in part to Bolshevik demands for division of the estates of aristocrats among the peasants. The peasants for the most part had no enthusiasm for communism, even if they knew what it was, but they remained favorably disposed towards the Bolsheviks or at least neutral in the civil wars of 1917-1921 because the Czarist forces fought for a return of the landed estates to their former owners. Had the Russian peasants supported the Czarist cause the Bolsheviks would almost certainly have been defeated and all subsequent history changed beyond imagination.[1]

---

1. Cf. p. 75.

The Economic Basis of National Power—The Mercantile System of the seventeenth and eighteenth centuries involved a deliberate attempt to increase state power by economic manipulation. Mercantilist statesmen believed that the total quality of trade in the world was fixed and were convinced that one country could increase its share of this total only by taking some of the trade of its rivals. This belief was the most important cause of several commercial wars involving England, France, and the Netherlands in the last half of the seventeenth century. According to another mercantilist doctrine colonies existed for the benefit of the mother country: to supply her with cheap raw materials and to provide a market for her manufactures. When this philosophy was applied by England to her American colonies, and was embellished by appropriate legislation (Sugar Act, Molasses Act, and Navigation Acts), it eventually became one of the causes of the American Revolution. Ironically, mercantilists assumptions about a fixed volume of trade and the mercantilist belief that victory in war is due to wealth in money, were largely incorrect; nonetheless they exerted a heavy influence on the national policies of most European countries for two centuries. Once more, what people think is true is often more important in its effects than what is actually true.

The Economic Basis of Ideals—The modern world is strongly influenced by economic ideas and ambitions. All the great revolutionary ideologies of modern times have some economic basis. One of the keynotes of nineteenth century liberalism was the demand for complete freedom from governmental interference in economic affairs. Socialism and communism arose primarily as protests against the long hours, low wages, wretched working conditions, and slums that were a part of the Industrial Revolution a century or more ago. Indeed one of the most striking evidences of the influence of economic changes upon historical developments is the sameness of the social problems produced in every Western country by the Industrial Revolution. In every country the social blight was quickly followed by the emergence of some brand of socialism as a proposed remedy.

The Fascist dictator Mussolini and the Nazi dictator Hitler gained much public support by their promises to solve the economic problems of Italy and Germany respectively. Both kept the promises to a degree, Hitler in particular bringing Germany out of the depression of the 1930's and restoring full employment by embarking on an enormous armaments' building program. Revolutionary movements in any part of the world since 1945 usually try to gain mass support by calling loudly for land reform and a general elevation of living standards. American political life has been heavily conditioned by memories of the depression of the 1930's. Whenever the country experiences, however slightly, a "recession" or "rolling readjustment" voices are immediately heard demanding federal spending programs to head off any possible new economic holocaust like that of a generation ago. It is sometimes alleged that the country fears depression more than war. The modern Welfare State on both sides of the Atlantic is the direct result of mass demands for a higher material standard of life and a greater degree of economic security. Unemployment Insurance, Accident Insurance, Old Age Pensions, and Social Security exist in some form in nearly all Western countries. They are only the particular manifestations of this general desire.

Technology as a Moulder of History—Perhaps the most obvious way history is influenced by economic factors is the limitations that have always been imposed on human activity by the contemporary level of technological development. The nature and results of warfare have always been severely limited by prevalent modes of military organization and the types of weapons available. As we have seen, when mounted knights dominated war they dominated medieval society. When weapons were invented that allowed common foot soldiers to defeat armored knights the aristocracy declined in every sphere of life. When national economies became sufficiently thriving and well organized that kings could hire, train, and supply armies of 100,000 to 300,000-men nations like the Netherlands and Sweden, whose small population allowed them to raise forces of only 30-50,000 men, sank permanently to the rank of second and third rate powers.

The conquests of Cortez and Pizarro in Mexico and Peru were made possible, to a considerable extent, by Spanish possession of two weapons unknown to the Indians, horses and firearms. The terrible destructiveness of twentieth century wars in human lives and property is due directly to the wedding of modern industrial technology to war. Every major modern war spurs research in chemistry, physics, ballistics, and mathematics in order to make the waging of war more efficient. Simultaneously, research in medicine is stimulated in order to patch up more of those directly affected by the first advances. The threat to all living things which is now posed by hydrogen bombs and various bacteriological weapons is due directly to technological "advances" since 1940.

The growth of the industrial factory system of production in the last 200 years, and particularly in the last 100, has probably changed man's manner of life more than any other phenomenon in history. The Industrial Revolution itself could not come about until certain technological problems were solved. Machine mass production required fine machine tools and interchangeable parts. These, in turn, could not be made without metals of superior quality and the invention, in the seventeenth century, of various instruments that enabled men to weigh and measure more precisely than ever before. Only when these technological advances had been made could the vast factories and sprawling industrial cities follow.

The extent to which the Industrial Revolution has shaped the course of modern history can hardly be exaggerated. The Western Great Plains of the United States could not be opened to agriculture until the invention of the Colt revolver, barbed wire, and railroads. Farming there could not be carried on successfully until the development of a variety of power mowers, reapers, threshers, and other machines that allowed a few men to harvest thousands of acres of grain. Before the Industrial Revolution the majority of mankind were farmers and agricultural yields were so low and precarious that the spectre of famine was ever present. In the twentieth century the combination of agricultural machinery, selective stock breeding, and extensive use of artificial fertilizers is beginning to reverse the situation in those countries that possess the machines and the techniques. Already in the United States a steadily dwindling number of farmers produce so much more food than a rapidly growing population can consume that chronic agricultural surpluses are an embarrassing and expensive problem.

Within the last century the Industrial Revolution has enabled myriads of people to live largely on canned food and to wear factory-made clothing. It has revolutionized the conduct of business by filling millions of offices with typewriters, computers, dictaphones, and similar devices. It has given man submarines, tanks, airplanes, and poison gas to enable him to fight his wars more efficiently. With the hydrogen bomb man has for the first time in history acquired a practical means of eliminating himself as a species.

No less remarkable have been the contributions of technology to medicine. No book would be more valuable and instructive than a first-rate *Medical Interpretation of History*. Nobody can have any idea of how much potential history never happened because of the great plague diseases that have decimated mankind since the beginning of time. It has been speculated, for instance, that malaria may have been a significant factor in the decline of ancient Assyria, Greece, and Rome; bilharzia of ancient Egypt. In nearly all history's major wars before the twentieth century far more soldiers died of disease than of battlefield injuries. Nobody knows how many Aristotles, Dantes, or da Vincis died in ages when childbirth losses of 50-80% were common. It has been only in the nineteenth and twentieth centuries that medical research has conquered most of the world's worst plagues, cut childbirth mortality dramatically, and made possible the most rapid population growth in recorded history. All this has been due directly to the knowledge, the instruments, and the techniques provided by modern science and industry.

The Industrial Revolution has brought the world a congeries of social problems it never knew before. The population of the world has at least trebled since 1800, a growth impossible in an agricultural society. The jobs provided by industry allowed hundreds of millions of people to secure the necessities of life where before they would have had no livelihood. Packing vast numbers into huge cities has raised problems of transportation, feeding, garbage disposal, and law enforcement that never before existed on a comparable scale. The automobile, moving pictures, radio, and television, have provided entirely new modes of entertainment for most of the population of the Western world. Television even threatens to alter drastically the character of politics in democratic countries. Regardless of ability, when candidates appear on television those who are "attractive personality types" enjoy a marked initial advantage over less photogenic, "sympathetic," or "dynamic" persons. Perhaps in the future only candidates with a Hollywood profile or a smile like a toothpaste ad can be elected? Finally, as noted before, the conditions of life in modern industrial society have directly given rise to the great revolutionary ideologies of modern times. Of these Nazism and Fascism caused World War II and communism now controls a third of the earth.

Technological Advances Follow Need—The inventions that are themselves the cause of technological change are often the product of keenly felt economic desires. The water frame, spinning jenny, and other devices that revolutionized textile manufacturing during the late eighteenth century were not the products of theoretical scientists. They were developed by "practical" textile mill owners and workers who were trying to find better and faster ways to weave cloth. Where no need is felt or no incentive for technological progress exists such progress is extremely slow or absent entirely. Water mills were known to the ancient Greeks and Romans but were seldom used because both societies were founded on slavery. Slaves have no incentive to devise better ways of doing things since such achievements gain them neither wealth nor fame nor freedom, but only some different task. Masters have no incentive either when slave labor is plentiful and cheap.

Likewise, if there seems no ready way to apply an invention or a revolutionary idea it is often stillborn. Leonardo da Vinci sketched plans for airplanes, submarines, and other mechanical devices, but nothing came of them because the sixteenth century had neither a pressing need for the machines nor any ready way to manufacture them. When further — desired — scientific advances were stymied by the need for new mathematical techniques in the late seventeenth century, however, it was more than coincidence that Leibniz and Isaac Newton should have developed calculus at the same time and in complete independence of each other.

Weaknesses of the Economic Interpretation—The economic interpretation of history, however, like every other one-track interpretation, has its limitations. To hold that history is determined entirely, or even mainly, by economic factors involves several assumptions of dubious validity. It assumes that people always know what their economic interests are; it assumes that human conduct is consistently motivated by rational considerations; it excludes free will; and it denies that men are moved significantly by nonmaterial factors. In brief, the economic interpretation of history, like other materialistic philosophies, proceeds more from a study of things than from a study of men. To begin with, even supposing that people always act in accord with their economic interest the fact remains that they frequently do not know what it really is. For generations many American businessmen have supported political candidates who opposed legislation designed to improve the wages and working conditions of labor. Ironically, the huge profits of contemporary American industry are due directly to the mass market that exists in the United States for consumer goods of every variety — and that mass market exists because the high wages paid to American labor provide a mass purchasing power unique in history. Millions are able to buy goods that in other countries only a handful of the wealthy can afford. The manufacturer makes a smaller profit per individual item but a larger over-all profit because of the increased volume of sales. Despite this easily understood and widely recognized American phenomenon most American businessmen still oppose any extension of its basic principle and most of their European counterparts continue to cling to a philosophy of high profits per article for a limited market.

As has been pointed out earlier,[1] the voting habits of people are influenced by loves, hates, cliches, ignorance, and irrational devotion to half truths, all of which have little to do with the economic determination of anything. In any practical situation economic considerations are always hopelessly jumbled with other factors anyway. It is often alleged that the imperialism of the late nineteenth century was economically motivated. To some degree this is true. The United States and European countries wanted parts of Africa, Asia, and the Pacific islands for the gold, diamonds, precious woods, rubber, tin, copra, and other products they contained, but they also wanted these places as coaling stations for their ships, sources of manpower to fill out armies, fields for missionary activity, and simply for prestige. Many a nineteenth century European statesman hastened to "prove" that a certain portion of Africa was economically valuable in order to make its acquisition seem reasonable and "practical" when the most pressing motive for taking it was mere national vainglory or a determination to prevent some rival country from getting the place.

Even if one grants, for the sake of argument, the Marxist contention that history records mostly a struggle for wealth between classes it only poses a further question, e.g., why do men desire wealth? In part, of course, for the physical comforts it brings; but also for the prestige accruing to it and for the power it brings over other men. In the business world the amassing of profits and wealth has always been the barometer of success, the way one "keeps score." One of the rewards of "success" is that the man or the class with wealth is always in an advantageous position to influence those who wield political authority, who lead the society intellectually, and who determine its ethical norms. The desire for power is one of the most deeply ingrained elements in the human character. It is one of the most constant factors in history, whether the locale be ancient Assyria, medieval Italy, or modern, and avowedly Marxist, Russia.

Differences In Time—Finally, the importance of economic considerations in history was much less in times past than now because society used to be dominated by kings and aristocrats, and their

---

1. Cf. p. 92.

class ideals were not economic. The European aristocracy lived primarily for honor and glory. Their ideals were chiefly military and chivalric. They thought mostly in terms of prestige and power for themselves, their families, and their nations, in approximately that order. Commerce they regarded as socially degrading. Merchants were scorned by aristocrats as an inferior social type. The nobility as a class so little understood the world of economics that many nobles lived perpetually on the brink of bankruptcy. Generations of European kings waged wars without a thought for the lives or interests of their peoples. They lavished money on wars, entertainments, and sumptuous courts, borrowed from anyone who would lend, and frequently did not even keep budgets. Kings like those of Prussia who enforced efficiency and Spartan economy upon every branch of their national administrations were extremely rare. Prodigality was accounted a distinctive princely characteristic, if not necessarily a virtue.

The rulers of the past were swayed by ideals which often conflicted with their economic interest. The sixteenth and seventeenth century kings of Spain drove out of their realm their most prosperous and industrious subjects, the Moriscos and Jews, because they did not wish to rule heretics and infidels. Louis XIV of France similarly expelled the thrifty Huguenots because his absolutist temperament could not bear the thought of tolerating subjects who refused to share his religious views. And how does one explain in economic terms the act of the Emperor Ferdinand II who, in 1620, signed the death warrants of Bohemian nobles while tears ran down his cheeks, and exclaimed, "I would sacrifice my life if it would make all these unbelievers believe."[1] Where does one find an economic explanation for the mad Italian campaign of 1494 undertaken by Charles VIII of France? Charles thought of himself as a new Alexander destined to reconquer the Byzantine Empire from the Turks and to be crowned Emperor of the New Rome in Constantinople? Economic factors often strongly influence the course of history but they no more control it exclusively than do great men or great ideas.

---

1. On another occasion the Emperor declared that he "would rather rule a desert than a land of heretics." Though his mood was plainly less compassionate, it is no easier to discern an economic motivation than in the first instance.

CHAPTER IX

MAN AND HIS PHYSICAL ENVIRONMENT

Geography and the Character of Civilization—Geography has been defined as a description of the world and its inhabitants in the order of space; history in the order of time. This is but a formal way of stating a truism: no nation or people can be properly understood without a knowledge of its surroundings and means of support. Local climatic conditions and the changing seasons regulate the choice of a people's food and clothing. The weather and the available raw materials normally determine the nature of buildings and building sites. It has even been contended that whether or not a civilization thrives and grows depends very largely on climatic conditions. The most recent and dramatic exposition of this view is that of the twentieth century philosopher of history Arnold Toynbee. It is a matter of fact that most of the world's thriving civilizations have grown up in the temperate zones. This (and much more) Toynbee accounts for by his famous "Challenge and Response" theory. In brief, his argument is that those peoples achieve, thrive, and advance most who live in conditions sufficiently difficult to challenge them to put forth their best efforts but not so harsh as to require the expenditure of all their energies merely to keep alive. People in the tropics have produced few great civilizations because the conditions of life are too easy to require men to put forth their best efforts. When building consists chiefly of piling palm leaves or jungle grass over wattles, when a few leaves or an animal skin suffices for clothing, and when feeding oneself is mostly a matter of picking fruit off trees or engaging in the simplest type of agriculture, it is difficult to be persuaded of the utility of working eight or ten hours a day to produce surpluses for export.

At the opposite pole Eskimos and Laplanders have produced little because their physical enviroment is so harsh that all their energies are exhausted by the effort to keep themselves alive.

The peoples of the temperate zone, however, have to work just hard enough to gain a livelihood that they acquire the habit and psychology of work and thrift, but not so hard that all their higher creative impulses are stifled by sheer toil and exhaustion like those of the inhabitants of the Arctic. The habits of working regularly and saving that are thus acquired in the temperate zones carry over into all human activities after the needs of mere existence are satisfied. The result has been the production of the world's great civilizations. To this whole theory the objection is sometimes raised that the civilizations of ancient Egypt and the Near East grew up in subtropical areas, but it is only fair to note that some geographers and archaeologists now think that these places were considerably colder in ancient times than at present.[1]

The influence, in particulars, of geography and climate upon a people's mode of life is easily observable. All nomadic societies tend to be much alike in their institutions and social habits. All of them develop in similar areas: desert, semi-desert, and dry tree-less plains. An island environment tends to produce a nation of seafarers like the modern British and Japanese. So does an in-hospitable homeland if the sea happens to be nearby. The Vikings who inhabited the forbidding rocky coasts of Norway had to depend upon the sea for a livelihood. Eventually they became a race of explorers and pirates who harried the coasts of Europe for genera-tions before settling in the tenth and eleventh centuries. It was chiefly the seafaring peoples of western Europe who explored and colonized North and South America and imparted their own civili-zation to it. In the late nineteenth century it was the same maritime European countries who explored and partitioned much of Africa.

Geographical considerations usually have a great deal to do with the way the earth is settled too. The earliest civilizations of which history has record grew up in Egypt and Mesopotamia. Both were in fertile river valleys where floods left rich soil on the land each year and where irrigation canals were easy to dig. Medieval towns usually grew up in geographically "logical" places: at fords in rivers, at the confluence of rivers or at their mouths, at crossroads, or in easily fortified places. Before the invention of the railroad or

---

1. The theories of Toynbee, here enormously oversimplified, are ex-pounded in fabulous detail in his ten volume *A Study of History,* for which there is an excellent abridgement in two volumes by D. C. Somervell. Though Toynbee's ideas have been challenged in many quarters and from many points of view, either the full length work or the abridged version is a fine thing for anyone to read once he has acquired some basic factual knowledge of history. Though Toynbee undoubtedly developed his theories first and then selected such facts as fit them, nonetheless *A Study of History* teems with unusual insights and thought-provoking analyses. No one can read it without learning much that he did not know before and being im-pelled to think afresh about his existing knowledge.

the building of roads worthy of the name the settlement of the New World proceeded chiefly up the valleys of navigable rivers.

Before the modern industrial age and basic occupation of an area was usually determined by the physical environment. If the land was mountainous or arid most of the population were herdsmen who lived off the products of their animals. If mineral deposits existed mining was the basic occupation. If fish were plentiful most of the people became fishermen. On fertile plains most of the people were farmers. The fur resources of Canada led many of the French there to become fur trappers and traders. The Dutch, living at the mouth of a great river system, on the sea, and along an important trade route, became one of the world's foremost commercial peoples.

Geography and War—Military history makes little sense unless one has some knowledge of geography, for military operations have always depended on the location of mountains, passes, rivers, swamps, plains, and lands rich enough to provide forage for horses. A few examples will illustrate this. Since prehistoric times Europe has been invaded repeatedly by Asiatics. The invaders have nearly always come across the plains of southern Russia immediately north of the Caspian Sea. The history of the world would undoubtedly have been considerably different, at least in details, had the gentle, rolling Ural Mountains which divide European and Asiatic Russia been a rugged, forbidding range like the Rockies or Himalayas. The two most thoroughly fought-over areas in Europe are the Po valley in northern Italy and the plains of Belgium. Each has been for centuries a rich area where loot was plentiful and military operations easy. The Belgian plain has the unhappy distinction of being the easiest and shortest invasion route from Germany to France or vice versa. The Po valley is the first place entered by any north European army coming through the Alpine passes and bent on the conquest of Italy. Likewise, it must be traversed by any army of a Mediterranean power being sent through the Alps to campaign in central Europe. Switzerland, by contrast, due to its masses of mountains, which favor the defense in war, and to its lack of easily exploitable wealth, has been overrun only once in the last six centuries. The conquest of Switzerland has simply never seemed worth the time and trouble to any modern warrior except Napoleon.

Russian military policy has for centuries been dictated by Russia's most obvious point of superiority over her European neighbors, her vast size. Whether opposing the Swedish king Charles XII, the

French emperor Napoleon I, or the German dictator Hitler, Russian strategy has been the same — withdraw slowly into the interior and trade space for time. Little by little the invader's supply lines grow longer and all his problems of communication, transportation, and feeding become more difficult. Then the terrible Russian winter descends. In the case of Charles XII, the Swedish army was so reduced by freezing and starvation in the winter of 1708-9 that the remnants were crushed at Poltava in the following spring. As Napoleon's army fled west out of Russia in 1812 it was nearly annihilated by the winter alone. The German army was never the same after facing simultaneously the severe winter of 1941-2 and Russian counterattacks. Interestingly, in the case of the German invasion, Stalin, perhaps in anticipation of a German invasion, in 1939 annexed the Baltic states and the eastern half of Poland, thereby gaining for Russia an additional 200 miles of defense in depth.

For centuries military campaigns anywhere in Europe were usually confined to six or seven months of the year for in winter the roads became impassable and food for horses difficult to find. Campaigns in the Netherlands were always very slow due to the boggy terrain and the numerous canals and rivers.

Not only geographical facts but geographical *conceptions* sometimes influence the military policies of nations. In France the belief was rooted for centuries that God had established the "natural boundaries" of France at the sea, the Pyrenees, the Jura, and the Rhine. Many French wars had as their main object to push the border of the country eastward to the Rhine. As late as the end of World War I in 1918 a considerable body of opinion in France favored annexation of the largely German-speaking areas west of the Rhine. During the nineteenth century when it was said to be the "Manifest Destiny" of the United States to expand it was conveniently discovered that our "natural western boundary" was the Pacific Ocean. There is much evidence that the famous "Mackinder Thesis" helped shape the military and political ambitions of the leaders of Nazi Germany. The basic idea originated with an English geographer, Sir Halford Mackinder. He thought that whoever could control an area which he called the "Heartland" (east-central Europe and western Russia) would be in a position to control the "World Island" (Europe, Asia, and Africa). Whoever controlled the "World Island" could eventually dominate the world. The German invasion of Russia in 1941 was, according to the Mackinder hypothesis, the logical first step towards eventual world domination — an effort to secure the "Heartland."

Indirect Geographical Influences—Physical environment has influenced the character and policies of nations in ways less obvious than those cited above but no less real or profound. An important reason why the nations of northwestern Europe have outstripped the Mediterranean states in the race for wealth and power is because iron, coal, and other raw materials essential for industrial developments are found in greater quantity and variety in the former states.[1]

The growth of England as a great power owes much to the sea. England's interest in naval affairs has always been due directly to her island position and, in the past century, to her need to import food as well. English domination of the seas in the eighteenth and nineteenth centuries grew directly from this. Domination of the seas, in turn, made possible the seizure of India and Canada from France in the eighteenth century and the acquisition of most of England's other colonial possessions in the nineteenth.

The growth of the English Parliament was indirectly stimulated by the same factor. Before the nineteenth century England's population was small compared with that of the other great powers of Europe. This alone would have made it nearly impossible for her to maintain simultaneously a navy strong enough to dominate the sea and a powerful standing army. Her island position dictated the primacy of naval interests. Fortunately, as long as the navy was kept strong invasion of England by a Continental power was impossible, and there was no longer any need to maintain a sizeable standing army. On the Continent, by contrast, every major state had to maintain a large standing army to defend itself against the aggressions of its neighbors. In the thirteenth and fourteenth centuries representative assemblies of various types grew up in most European countries. On the Continent when differences developed between these bodies and kings the kings usually had strong military forces at their disposal which could be employed as a final argument. Consequently, no parliamentary body in a major Continental country played an unbroken, meaningful role in that nation's history from the thirteenth century to the twentieth. In England, however, kings never had standing armies to use argainst parliaments.

---

1. This theme is developed in some detail in Amintore Fanfani's interesting book, *Catholicism, Protestantism, and Capitalism.*

When quarrels between King and Parliament became so acute in the seventeenth century that both sides resorted to force each started on the same footing militarily and the Parliamentary party won the war. Thus Parliamentary influence, which had existed continuously since the thirteenth century, became dominant in the government of England. The difference between the fate of parliaments in Britain and on the Continent can be viewed from another geographical angle too. Continental states always needed strong royal authority and regular governmental income. The wrangling and delays that are an integral part of parliamentary government posed a greater threat to the physical safety of Continental states than to England. The reasons are geographical. The Continental states were land powers, located side by side. England was protected by that priceless twenty-mile ditch, the English Channel.

The ancient Greeks were prone to incessant quarreling and were notoriously unable to achieve political unity. One reason was nothing more than the terrain of Greece. The country is a series of steep mountain ranges and narrow valleys which serve to break up the population into small enclaves and to make communication between them difficult.

In more recent times isolationist sentiment among great powers has been strongest in nineteenth century Japan, nineteenth and twentieth century England, and the United States, places far removed geographically from that home of major wars, Continental Europe. In World War I the countries on the periphery of Europe, Spain in the southwest and the Scandinavian states in the north, were able to remain neutral. In World War II out-of-the-way Spain, Portugal, and Sweden managed to escape participation.

Exaggeration of Geographical Influences—Like every other factor which influences history the importance of geography can be overrated. The eighteenth century philosophe Montesquieu was prone to discover geographical and climatic explanations for phenomena of every sort. The nineteenth century historian Henry T. Buckle went so far as to ascribe the prevalence of "superstition" in Portugal, Spain, and Italy to the frequency of earthquakes and volcanic eruptions in those lands. Here, as elsewhere, one must never forget that though man may be strongly influenced by his environment he is not its helpless slave. Logically, considering the pertinent geographical, climatic, financial, and military factors, Washington should have surrendered at Valley Forge, but he and his men hung on with dogged determination and lived to win the

American Revolution. Logically, the ancient Greek city-states should have reacted the same way in any major crisis for their people were of the same racial stock and their geographical environment was very similar. Yet when faced with the problem of overpopulation Sparta reacted by becoming a militaristic and imperialistic state, Corinth by establishing colonies overseas in Sicily and Southern Italy, and Athens by developing handicraft industries to produce export goods and inventing democratic political institutions to pacify the classes engaged in these industries. The element of human will power, even sheer caprice, must never be discounted in history. According to all geographical logic ancient Rome should have been a mighty naval power. Italy lies astride the Mediterranean, in ancient times the world's foremost waterway. Rome's empire stretched for thousands of miles along both shores of the Mediterranean and for additional hundreds of miles northwest and southeast of it. Yet Rome built great navies only when particular problems required them: to wage the Carthaginian wars of the second and third centuries B.C. and to combat Mediterranean pirates in the first century B.C. As soon as a particular menace had passed the navy was allowed to run down. One can only conclude that, geography or not, the Romans were simply not particularly interested in naval affairs.

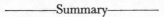

————Summary————

Any discussion of historical causation inevitably comes to one general conclusion: complex phenomena have more than one cause. It is always easier to assign one cause to an event than to try to weigh the relative importance of several. Oftentimes, of course, one cause is considerably more important than any of the others; but, as a general rule, one comes nearer the truth if he looks for several factors in a given situation instead of only one. Human affairs are seldom as simple as they seem. The more one learns about anything the more complex he finds it.

As the reader of this book is aware, the same events or circumstances have been used repeatedly to illustrate several different points. The career of Mohammed has been cited to indicate the importance of both ideas and individual men in history. The French Revolution has been employed to show the importance of ideas (the ideas of Liberty, Equality, and Fraternity inspired the French army in its campaigns), men (Louis XVI, Mirabeau, and Napoleon), technology and organization (eighteenth century military reforms made possible the Revolutionary and Napoleonic military conquests), and the persistent sameness of much in human affairs (the French administration ran the country much the same after the Revolution as before it). Examples have been taken from different aspects of the First World War to illustrate nearly every major point made in this book: Bismarck's alliance system and the railroad timetables to show how men sometimes seem but the puppets of forces beyond their control, the assassination of Franz Ferdinand to point up the difference between a basic and a superficial cause, Wilsonian propaganda to indicate the force of ideas, and military aspects of the war to demonstrate the growing importance of industrial technology. Various phases of the history of warfare have been discussed to exemplify the importance of men, ideas, organizations, the level of technology, and geography, in the conduct of military operations and, therefore, indirectly, as determinants in human history. Lastly, in all historical situations there is another factor, not easily analyzed but invariably present: the craving of human beings for domination over others; the ambition to direct, control — rule.

It is all ultimately reducible to what one historian has called the only law in history, the law of multiple causation.[1]

---

1. Carl Gustavson, *A Preface to History.* This excellent book discusses many of the same matters as the present volume, though in a different way. Any beginner in history will find it well worth his time to read.

CHAPTER X

DOING A TERM PAPER

Why Write a Paper at All?—In most history courses of the survey type a research paper is required. Many students regard this as the most onerous part of the course, a particularly fiendish tyranny practiced upon them, and for no discernible reason, by their teachers. They appear to think that, somehow or other, the paper is done for the benefit of the teacher. Actually, there are a number of excellent reasons why term papers are required in survey courses.

1) A person goes to college, presumably, to become educated. Nobody can call himself truly educated unless he can write clearly and correctly. One learns to write respectably in the same way he learns to do anything else: by practice.

2) A part of history is learning facts about the past. Another part is learning how historians discover those facts, think about them, interpret them, and mould them into history books. It is for this reason that the student is required to take notes in a special way, prepare his bibliography cards in a certain manner, and observe specified rules of form when doing his paper. No paper of 1000-2000 words can involve more than a tiny fraction of the research that goes into the writing of an entire book, but a paper of even this short length, if prepared carefully from six to a dozen sources, will give the beginning student some experience in the problems of assembling historical data and practice in the correct and systematic expression of his ideas.

3) If one does a good paper on a certain topic he acquires a knowledge of at least one small area of history that is much fuller and more detailed than the type of knowledge derived from survey courses generally.

4) Many college courses, in a variety of fields, require term papers. To do a serious research paper, following all the rules of form, in a beginning history course, is good practice for what will come later.

Here, as elsewhere in the study of history, begin by taking a common sense view of the matter. Suppose one's paper is to be a study of the defeat of the Spanish Armada. Start by reading all the

125

material that can be found on the episode until all the facts and all the interpretations that have been placed on those facts are thoroughly understood. Then sit down and write a clear, direct account of the matter that would be understood by a person of ordinary intelligence and information, citing the sources on which the paper is based. The whole process has three steps: 1) collect the information, 2) think the problem through, and 3) write it out in your own words in a manner in which you would like to read it if it was written by someone else.

Rules for the Preparation of a Term Paper

1. *Selection of the Topic*—Normally, essay topics are selected by the instructor, though sometimes the student is allowed to select his own.

2. *Preliminary Readings*—Once the topic has been chosen the student should begin by acquainting himself with it in a general way. Topics usually deal with relatively minute portions of history about which a beginner normally does not have much knowledge. If the student begins by reading an entire book on the matter he often finds himself bewildered by a mass of details and quite unable to distinguish what is of basic importance from what is merely explanatory or peripheral. Hence it is a good idea to begin by reading brief summaries of the matter in order to get its main features in mind, and then to gradually work into the details.

A good practice is to begin by reading the pertinent section of the textbook. Usually this will not be more than a few pages, sometimes no more than a paragraph or even a couple of lines. The next step should be to read a few encyclopedia articles about the subject, or biographical sketches of persons prominently associated with it. This will increase the extent of one's general knowledge of the matter. Among the better encyclopedias found in any college library are *Encyclopaedia Britannica, Encyclopedia Americana, Dictionary of American Biography, Dictionary of National Biography* (relates to the British Isles only), *Encyclopedia of the Social Sciences, Catholic Encyclopedia,* and *Dictionary of American History.* Use only the better encyclopedias. There are many reference works which have short articles written on the popular level. There is nothing in these books that is not treated better in the ones named above.

Once one has gotten a good "encyclopedia knowledge" of his subject he should then go to the card catalog and get books that deal with it. By now he should be able to understand a detailed, minute discussion of any aspect of the problem.

3. *Preparation of the Bibliography*—A bibliography should now be compiled. (A bibliography is a list of all the materials consulted in the preparation of the paper.) On cards or slips of paper, the student should indicate the books or articles dealing with his particular topic, *using a separate card for each title.* The reason for the last admonition is that in any research paper or book the bibliography is listed alphabetically. In some books and dissertations the bibliographical entries run into the hundreds. If one put down many titles haphazardly, with several on any given sheet of paper, he would waste more time shuffling paper when the time came to append the bibliography to his finished work than it would have taken to put each item on a separate card in the first place. This would not be a problem in a short paper where only a few sources are used, but one of the purposes of the paper is to teach the student the *research method* and thus bibliographical entries should be put on separate cards — the best practice in serious, lengthy research.

Each bibliography card must contain 1) the name of the author, 2) the title of the book, with place of publication, publisher, and date of publication (in that order), and 3) a brief statement of the use which can be made of the book in the preparation of the essay. If the student follows these directions he will have all the information he needs to prepare the Final Bibliography for his paper when the paper itself is completed. If he does not do this he will have to go back to the library and get the books again in order to get the bibliographical information that must be included in the Bibliography of the finished paper. By then someone else will probably have checked out the needed books.

In the case of materials taken from an encyclopedia the bibliography card should show 1) the name of the author, if the article is signed, 2) the title of the article, 3) the name of the encyclopedia, 4) the edition (most encyclopedias have gone through many editions), 5) the volume number, and 6) the pages on which the article appears.

In the case of magazines or newspapers the card should show the author, title of article, name of magazine or paper, date of publication and pertinent pages.

In the case of a work, different portions of which have been done by different authors, the card should indicate 1) the author of the *chapter you used* (not the editor of the whole book or series), 2) the title of that chapter (in quotation marks), 3) the title of the book (underlined), and 4) place of publication, publisher, and date. Typical bibliography card:

> Wagenknecht, Edward. *The Seven Worlds of Theodore Roosevelt.*
> (New York: Longmans, Green and Co., 1958)
> Has a good chapter on Roosevelt's thought about war and peace,
> pp. 247-287.

A bibliography can be built up in several ways. There are usually book lists at the end of each major section of a textbook. Sometimes there are lists at the end of each chapter. Encyclopedia articles will sometimes cite references in the body of an article: nearly all will include a few at the end of the article. Many good leads can be obtained by glancing over the footnotes and extensive bibliographies which are invariably included in scholarly books. A book that deals with one's subject will probably list other useful works in its bibliography section. Especially recommended for their bibliographies are the *Cambridge Ancient History, Cambridge Medieval History, Cambridge Modern History,* the *Rise of Modern Europe* series (edited by William L. Langer and comprising many volumes on European history from 1250 to the twentieth century), the *Chronicles of America* series, and the *American Nation* series.

Last, and most important, consult the card catalog in the library. Here some resourcefulness must be displayed. Suppose the title of one's topic is "The Spanish Armada." Start by looking under "Armada." There may or may not be an entire book written about the subject. If there is not don't go away in despair (or elation), thinking that no material exists. Any history of the British navy would almost certainly contain material about the Armada since its defeat was one of the great events of British naval history. Most general naval histories would also have references. Any history of England would have at least a short reference to the Armada. If it is a multivolume history the volume that covers the late sixteenth century would probably have a lengthy reference. Who was the ruler of England at the time? Elizabeth I. Any biography of her would contain references. Who commanded the victorious English fleet? Howard, Frobisher, Drake, and Hawkins. Perhaps they wrote their memoirs? If not, surely somebody has written biographies of one or all of them. Then consider the Spanish side. Any Spanish naval history, any general history of Spain, any biography of Philip II (king of Spain at the time), the memoirs (if he wrote any) of the Duke of Medina Sidonia, who commanded the Armada, or any biographies of Medina Sidonia, would contain useful material. One can nearly always find information about virtually anything in a library if he will but exercise a little ingenuity.

If the subject concerns something that has taken place in the last century or so there will almost certainly be magazine articles about it. To look for materials of this sort consult *Reader's Guide to Periodical Literature* or *Poole's Index to Periodical Literature*. For recent history the files of the *New York Times, Time, Newsweek, U.S. News and World Report*, and similar publications will nearly always have information.

A subject from almost any period in history will have had articles about it published at some time or other in learned journals. Among many of these the *American Historical Review, Mississippi Valley Historical Review, English Historical Review, History, History Today, Cambridge Historical Journal, Catholic Historical Review, Journal of Central European Affairs, Review of Politics*, and *Journal of Modern History*, are well known. Periodicals of this sort are usually indexed.

4. *Note Taking*—Notes should be taken regularly as the source materials for the paper are read. The notes should include anything that might be of value in the preparation of the paper. Do not be alarmed if the stack of notes grows high. It is not uncommon to accumulate ten times as much material in notes as ever finds its way into the finished paper. It is much easier to throw away a note that was not needed than to go back to the library and rummage around trying to find some bit of information or some quotation that was not taken down at the time but was needed afterward.

Students frequently wonder why they have to take notes at all. Now, to be sure, for short papers based on only a few sources, it would be easier to get four or five relevant books, read around in them, spread them all out on a table, thumb back and forth through them, take a sentence here and an idea there, paste them together with an occasional sentence of one's own, and eventually construct a paper-of-sorts. No serious research can be done this way, though, for any lengthy or detailed work requires the use of many different materials, often from several libraries. Nobody's memory is good enough to recall masses of details accurately for any length of time and libraries will not normally let one keep books for long periods.

Moreover, it would be hopeless to try to write a paper from thirty or forty sources in the manner described above. The only way serious research can be done is by taking notes as one goes along. It is the only way great quantities of information can be accurately reduced to usable dimensions. Remember, one of the purposes of doing a paper at all is to learn the *research method*. Hence, notes should be taken carefully for even the shortest papers. Notes may take one of several forms:

A) A summary in the student's own words of the contents of a paragraph, page, or chapter. This is by far the commonest type of note. The bulk of one's notes should always be of this type. If the source material deals with the subject of the paper only in a general way it may be possible to summarize several pages in a few sentences or a short paragraph. If the material is immediately pertinent to the subject the notes should be much fuller. *How* much fuller is a matter of judgment: but don't forget, one takes notes for his own use. Anything that might go into the final paper ought to be taken down.

b) A direct quotation of a passage which seems of special interest or importance. This ought to be done sparingly since it is not advisable to clutter a paper with many direct quotations. This will be explained later.

c) A simple statement (reminder) that something of interest is to be found at a certain point in a specific book or article. Notes of this type should be rare. If the material really is of interest it would normally be better to take notes on it when one reads it. Occasionally, however, one may own books relevant to the subject or may have easy access at any time to relevant materials. In these cases a note of the "reminder" type may save some needless note-taking of the regular sort.

A sample subject note on our hypothetical topic, "The Spanish Armada," ought to be something like the following. At the top of the note card there should be a brief statement of what aspect of the subject the note concerns: e.g., "Spanish Battle Plans." Then should come the body of the note. At the end the source should *always* be indicated. It is not necessary to write the author, book title, and bibliographical information on every note card. Keep all of this information somewhere on *one card*. Use some sort of abbreviation or key to identify individual note cards derived from any one source. *Every* note card, however, *without exception must* contain the *page number* or *numbers* in the source from which the material in the note is derived. The reason for this is that if foot-notes are to be of much use to the reader they have to refer to a *specific page or two* in a source. (A reader is not helped if you tell him that a certain point may be verified if he will but read pp. 98-184 in one of your sources.) When one is taking notes he has no way of knowing how and when he is going to cite footnotes when he writes his paper weeks later. Hence he should always keep track of the *exact page* from which every bit of his note material is drawn.

In all cases notes should be taken on small cards or small pieces of paper. Write only on one side of the card and put only one idea on each card. There are sound reasons for all these injunctions. Small cards are easier to handle than whole sheets of paper. If one writes on both sides of a card and puts several ideas on a single card he may save some space but when he gets ready to write his paper he will spend far more time shuffling cards, turning them over and over, and crossing out parts of them as he uses bits of material here and there, than he would have had he used more cards to start with, written on only one side, and used a separate card for each different idea. It takes more cards but it saves time in the long run. Moreover, if ideas are kept separate and writing is only on one side it is easy to read through the note cards and arrange them in the order that will be followed when writing the essay.

5. *Preparation of the Topical Outline*—The student then should think over his topic as it appears in his subject notes and prepare a short topical outline (about half a page) indicating in the proper order the points he intends to bring out in his essay. If he finds that he does not have enough information on some aspects of the essay further research on that point should be done before the writing begins.

6. *Preliminary Approval*—Bibliography cards, subject notes, and topical outline must be ready for submission to the instructor about a month after the beginning of the semester. If the topic is ap-proved, the student may then begin to write his essay.

7. *Writing the Essay*—After the student has completed his re-search he should read through all his notes and preliminary out-lines, think about the whole problem, arrange his notes in the order in which he expects to use them, and begin writing the essay. He should endeavor to tell the reader what he has found or concluded, as clearly, simply, and straightforwardly as he can. The following directions and advice should be heeded.

A. Make sure that the title of the essay accurately describes its contents. Don't entitle a paper, "Leo III and the Iconoclast Controversy," and then write about Leo's plans for the general administrative reorganization of the Byzantine Empire.

B. In a short essay avoid any but the briefest introduction. Get to the point quickly and be careful not to digress. If the paper is five pages long the introduction and conclusion should not normally exceed half a page each, at most.

C. The purpose of writing history is to tell the truth as nearly as possible. The first attribute of any historical essay is accuracy and reliability. If this can be combined with elegance of expression, engaging figures of speech, wit, irony, and the other ingredients of fine writing, so much the better, but accuracy must always take precedence over the fine phrase and the striking adjective if their use in any way distorts the truth.

D. The essay should reflect a calm, detached spirit. National, political, religious, or class convictions must never be allowed to destroy the objectivity of the essay. It is the historian's business to describe what happened, how it came to happen, and what resulted from the said happenings. It is not his business to champion democracy against dictatorship, Protestants against Catholics, or laborers against owners. Naturally, he will have personal convictions about these and similar matters but they do not belong in writings that purport to be history.

E. Weigh the evidence. Do not be surprised if puzzles are encountered in research, or conflicting accounts, or radically different interpretations of events. Sometimes accounts of events are changed markedly because new information becomes available that was unknown to earlier writers. Virtually any issue in the past which has provoked a controversy has been written about by special pleaders for every party to it. Their interpretations of events and even their accounts of *what happened* often vary widely. Finally, opinions will always differ about what *is* really significant in any given situation and what is the proper interpretation of it. Every professional historian has encountered innumerable problems of this sort.

When sources disagree it is sometimes possible to resolve the conflict, and sometimes not. If one is faced with such a conflict he should begin by reading as many other accounts of the events in question as he can find. If most writers incline to one view, and only one or a distinct minority hold out for something different, the majority is apt to be nearer the truth, though this is by no means *necessarily* the case. It is always possible that one man might be right and 100 wrong, though this is not normally so. Sometimes it is possible to find out that one party was in a better position to know the facts than another or that his experience and judgment were such that one would expect his interpretation to be reliable. Sometimes the writer's own common sense inclines him to one side or the other in such cases, though this is, of course, by no means an infallible guide.

If differences of interpretation can be clearly traced to the sectarian or party interest of one of the writers, then the views of the other should normally be preferred. If the interpretations reflect party interest on both sides probably the truth lies somewhere in the middle. If each version seems to possess about the same degree of probability just let it go at that and suspend judgment. It is not possible to resolve every difference. To take sides when the facts do not warrant it, just to "come to a decision," may be creative writing but it is worthless as history. The best solution, in practice, is to include in the body of the paper what seems the most reasonable and likely version or interpretation of a controversial episode; then cite a footnote giving the sources for this version, the sources that disagree, and the reasons for their disagreement.

F. Be impersonal in a formal paper. Do not begin, "In this paper I am going to prove to you . . . ." Begin, "The purpose of this essay is to demonstrate . . . ." Do not write, "Now you see that the decline of Napoleon's empire was due to . . . ." Write, rather, "From the foregoing it is clear that the decline was due to . . . ."

G. Always identify any unfamiliar persons, terms, titles, offices, and the like. Remember, it is your business to enlighten the reader, not to confuse him or make things difficult for him. Everyone has read exasperating books full of a bewildering assortment of persons and names, none of which are identified. Persons or designations of the first magnitude need not be specifically identified but all below it should be. Reference in the essay to Julius Caesar, George Washington, the British Parliament, or the Papacy need not be accompanied by identifications. If names of this sort are unfamiliar to the reader he ought not to be reading the essay in the first place. However, references to Camille Morand, Rudolf von Kluttzhof, Sylvester Watson, or the Order of the Golden Fleece, should always be followed by a description of the person or term since the reader cannot reasonably be expected to be as knowledgeable in these cases as about George Washington. The description need not be long. Merely mention that Camille Morand was Governor of New

Hampshire, a general in the Swiss army, a French newspaperman of socialist sympathies, or whatever the case might be.

H. Avoid excessive use of quotations. To be sure, a direct quotation *does* have its place. If a given situation is summed up briefly and succinctly, or with engaging wit, or in some particularly apt and forceful manner, it is better to put the quotation in your essay than to try to retell the matter yourself. This is very much the exception, however. Nine times out of ten it is preferable to use one's own words. Never use long quotations of half a page or more. Long quotations clot the flow of the narrative and are more apt to irritate the reader than to please him. Ask yourself: how many times have I encountered long quotations in a book and skipped over them in order to get on with the narrative?

When one begins to write it is wise not only to forswear long quotations but to avoid writing directly from one's own notes as well. The reason is that the sight of a certain description staring at one from a note card frequently induces a paralysis of the imagination. One simply cannot think of another way to say a thing than the way it appears on the card. Since what is on the note card is apt to be a close paraphrase of the original source, if one transfers the phraseology of his note cards to his essay the essay will read as though it had been virtually copied. It is much better to read all one's notes for a given section of the paper, think about the matter, put the notes aside, and then write the account in one's own words. *Then* refer to the note cards again and correct inaccuracies or add any information of importance that was omitted. Writing directly from notes tends to ruin the literary quality of a paper, too, for the finished product becomes a mixture of the styles of all its sources. It has a choppy, inconsistent quality, sounding here like one of the sources and there like another one. If the notes are read and then put aside, and the paper written without looking at them every minute, the whole paper will at least be in the writer's *own* style, for better or worse.

I. Anything which would normally be italicized in a printed book should be underlined or placed in quotation marks: e.g., the names of ships (*Titanic*, "Lusitania"), or newspapers (*New York Times*), or magazines ("Harper's"), or the titles of books (*Tobacco Road*).

J. Be careful of errors in composition, misspelled words, faulty grammar, and incorrect punctuation. As a matter of pride, a person should always write as well as he is able. An essay that is sloppily written and full of grammatical blunders ought to be failed as readily as one with historical inaccuracies. Among the commoner faults are failure to capitalize consistently, dividing words at places other than the ends of syllables, and leaving one letter dangling at the end of a line. Also, spell out numbers of one or two digits, but use figures for others.

K. Avoid antiquated secondary works. More recent works are sometimes based on information unknown to earlier authors and, oftener than not, they will be less prone to partisanship. Wherever possible, use secondary works written within the last generation.

L. Writing well. Real literary excellence is to some degree a gift, but anyone can improve his writing in two ways: a) practice, and b) reading good writing by others. The latter is an important reason why the habit of reading "quality" newspapers and magazines should be cultivated. Some such publications are *Harper's, Atlantic Monthly, The New York Times, Manchester Guardian Weekly,* and *Saturday Review.* Aside from the value of the information found in these and similar publications, their literary quality is excellent. If a person of any intelligence reads good writing with some consistency eventually his own style will improve.

Aside from this general advice there are a number of specific ways in which one can improve his writing.

1) Try to write so clearly that no sane person could possibly misunderstand you. When you have finished writing the essay read it over slowly and carefully. If *you* have to read anything a second time to be sure of its meaning it is quite certain that the matter will be less clear still to someone else. Rewrite it.

2) Write chiefly in short, direct sentences. A person of exceptional literary skill can employ many long, involved sentences and still convey his message clearly and attractively, but most people cannot. Any essay should contain some lengthy sentences, of course, otherwise it sounds abrupt and choppy, but clarity is usually best achieved if the majority are fairly short. Whenever sentences begin to run consistently to three or four lines look for ways to divide them and simplify the narrative.

3) Write as economically as possible. Just to write at great length is not necessarily a virtue. If one understands a subject thoroughly he can condense it and still express it adequately. Much vagueness and verbosity is due not to immense learning but to lack of understanding. One should write at sufficient length to explain the subject thoroughly, but no more.

4) Be sure that what is put on paper represents the thought that is in your mind. Remember, the reader cannot read your mind; he can only read what you put on paper. If you do not use words explicitly and precisely, he is bound to misunderstand you. A very common fault among students is to use as synonyms words that have only a *roughly similar* meaning. For example, "large," "many," "great," "important," and "impressive," have vaguely similar meanings but by no means can they be used interchangeably.

5) Eliminate clichés. Few things are more tedious than reading an essay full of tired old figures of speech that one has encountered scores of times in the past. Use your imagination. Try to think of new ways to express familiar ideas. Don't forget the synonym dictionary. It has rescued many a writer whose imagination was stranded on one word. Also, do not repeat a word soon after its first usage. Look for a synonym.

6) Don't start sentences with conjunctions. Persons who write for a living become arbiters of literary fashion and break rules as they choose, but the beginner oftener needs practice in observing long-standing usages than in breaking them.

7) Be consistent with tenses. Write either in the present or the past tense throughout the paper. The past is ordinarily preferable since the events took place in the past. In any case, do not wander aimlessly from one to the other, saying in one place, "Charles Martel then *took* command of the army and *marched* north," and in another, "Martel now *sees* that the Saracen forces *will be* too much for him."

8) Do not be alarmed at the prospect of rewriting. Most experienced or professional writers rewrite many times to get just the right polish and the correct shade of meaning. Lord Macaulay, one of the great literary stylists of the nineteenth century, once said, "What labor it is to make a tolerable book, and how little readers know how much trouble the ordering of the parts has cost the author."[1]

9) Self-criticism. It is easy to see flaws in someone else's work but nobody is a good critic of his own. One can become a fair critic of his own writing, however, if he will put it aside for a time and read it after it has "gotten cold." Try reading something that you have written several weeks or months or even years ago. It can be positively embarrassing! Errors and clumsy phrases of every

---

1. *Journal*, 1854, p. 377.

sort strike the eye immediately. Not infrequently one mutters to himself in half-disbelief, "Did *I* do that?" The moral is that, whenever possible, prepare a written assignment well in advance of the due date. Lay it aside and do not look at it for several days or weeks, as time permits. Then, shortly before it is to be submitted, read it over. Normally one will find mistakes and infelicitous phrases that would have escaped his attention had he read the paper only immediately after it was written.

If the student heeds these injunctions, and particularly if he reads "quality" writing with some regularity, he will usually begin to see improvement in his own writing. Few experiences are more rewarding.

Rules for the Form of the Essay

1. *Margins*—The margin on all sides of the page should be approximately one inch, not less.

2. *Page numbering*—Page one should be numbered in the center, at the bottom of the page. All other pages are numbered in the upper right hand corner. The Bibliography page is numbered just like a page in the regular text of the paper. Use Arabic numerals.

3. *Spacing*—Double space the regular text of the paper throughout. Footnotes, bibliography items, and quotations of more than three lines are single spaced in a manner explained below.

4. *Punctuation and Capitalization*—Follow standard rules. In case of doubt consult your English handbook.

5. *Indentation*—Paragraphs must be indented uniformly. See Rule 6 for the indentation of quotations which exceed three lines.

6. *Direct Quotations*—All quotations from books, articles, newspapers, or other persons must be enclosed in quotation marks, and the source indicated in a footnote. If the quotation is more than three lines in length it should be boxed: e.g., indented five spaces on *both sides* and *single spaced*. This arrangement allows the quotation marks to be dropped since the fact that the material is a direct quotation is apparent from the indentation and single spacing alone.

7. *Footnotes*—The purpose of citing footnotes is to aid the reader. A footnote informs the reader from what source or sources certain information has been derived, it provides him with a guide if he wishes to read further on the subject, and it enables him to check the accuracy of the writer's assertions and interpretations. When to

cite footnotes is to some degree a matter of judgment, but the following principles ought to be kept in mind as a guide.

A. All direct quotations of any kind from any source *must* be footnoted. There are no exceptions. Direct quotations should be used sparingly, as explained earlier, but if they are used they must *always* consist of the *exact* words of the source. To use only the approximate words of the source and then enclose them in quotation marks lays one open to the charge of misquoting and distorting the meaning of the original.

B. When the work of a writer is paraphrased, that should be indicated in a footnote. (It is seldom a good practice to paraphrase, as this is not far removed from plagiarism. It is preferable to think about the facts and ideas found in a source and then to express them in one's own words.)

C. A footnote should be cited if one introduces obscure or little known information. For instance, if one read parts of tens books for his paper and found a certain bit of pertinent information in only one of them this should ordinarily be footnoted.

D. Any technical or highly detailed information should be footnoted. Suppose the subject is a naval battle and one has occasion to relate that a certain ship has a crew of 350, was 488 feet long, carried seventy-seven guns of a certain caliber, had four-inch oak deck planking, and ninety sails of various sizes. Nobody carries information of this sort around in his head. The reader should be told from whence the author has acquired it.

E. Whenever a motive, opinion, or state of mind is ascribed to someone mentioned in the paper a footnote should be cited. The reason is that these are matters about which absolute certitude is impossible. No one can read someone else's mind and divine his thoughts beyond possibility of error.

F. If sources differ in their interpretation of events what seems the most likely version should be followed in the text. Then a footnote should be cited indicating this fact and also informing the reader that other writers disagree in certain respects.

G. If one uses material from a primary source a footnote is normally cited. (The difference between primary and secondary sources is explained below in the *Bibliography* section.)

H. Footnotes should be cited occasionally to guide the reader to the principal sources of information used in preparing the paper.

I. Footnotes are freqeuntly used for comments by the author

which would not fit readily into the main text. They are sometimes employed to insert interesting information that is related to some point in the text but is not sufficiently important to be put into the text itself. They may also be used to refer the reader to other parts of the paper.

J. Footnotes should *not* be cited when relating mere routine information about which there is no doubt or controversy and which is readily available in any number of places in the library. Do not footnote some statement like, "Charlemagne was crowned Holy Roman Emperor on Christmas Day, 800 A.D." Such information is available in any textbook.

K. How many footnotes to put on a page is a matter of judgment. Two, three, or four is perhaps a general average but the number depends mostly on the subject of the paper. If the paper is largely descriptive and the facts contained in it are not in dispute not many footnotes are needed. If the paper concerns a controversial subject or one about which there is little knowledge and much conjecture, footnotes should be more plentiful.

The following rules should be observed when citing footnotes.

a) Footnotes should be at the bottom of the same page as the material to which they refer in the text of the paper.

b) The number cited in the text of the paper comes *after* the material referred to, not before it.

c) Number the footnotes consecutively from the beginning to the end of the essay. Do not start with "one" again on each page.

d) Do not cite footnotes from textbooks. The reason is that it is the nature of a textbook to cover a long period and a great variety of subjects rather sketchily. Necessarily, the author of a textbook has to discuss many subjects about which he has less than an expert's knowledge. Hence a textbook should not be cited to clinch an argument or prove a point.

e) After the last line of the regular double-spaced text of the paper, double space again and type a solid line for about 15-20 spaces from the left margin of the paper. Then double space again and begin to put in the footnotes. Footnotes are all single spaced. There is no double space between separate footnotes. Each separate footnote is indented five spaces on its first line, in the same way as a new paragraph is indented.

Following are samples of the commoner types of footnotes, with directions for their proper punctuation.

A. The commonest type of footnote is the reference to a one volume book written by one author.

1. George Jones, *History of Rome*, p. 68.

Note that the author's first name comes first. The footnote contains the name of the author, name of the book, small "p" to indicate the page, and the exact page or pages from which the information was obtained. If the information had come from pages 68 *and* 69 the citation would have been "pp." 68-69.

B. A work by one man which runs to more than one volume is done as follows. The only difference from example one (above) is that the small "p" for the page is omitted when a volume number appears. The volume number itself is given in Roman numerals.

2. J. W. Wilson, *Life of Julius Caesar*, II, 543.

C. Some books are cooperative works in which different chapters or sections are written by different authors. Such a one is the *Cambridge Modern History*. In these cases cite first the author of the chapter or article *you used* (not the editor of the whole book or series); followed by the chapter title in quotation marks, the chapter number, the title of the whole work (underlined), volume, and page.

3. J. R. Moreton Macdonald, "The Terror," Chapter XII, *The Cambridge Modern History*, VIII, 338-9.

D. If the author of a portion of a cooperative work cannot be identified, the footnote should begin with the chapter, article, or division title. This is quite common in the case of encyclopedia articles, some of which are signed with a full name, some with initials, and some not at all. If the name or initials are there, use them. If not, begin with the title of the article.

4. "Black Death," *Encyclopaedia Britannica*, (11th ed.), III, 552.

Note that the small "p" is not used in the case of encyclopedia or magazine articles.

E. A footnote referring to an article in a periodical contains the author's name, the title of the article in quotation marks, the title of the periodical, the volume number, date of publication, and page or pages.

5. Richard K. Morris, "Taxation in Medieval France," *American Historical Review*, XXVI, (1927), 175.

F. If the reference is to a collection of documents, cite the author of the pertinent document, the name of the document, the editor of the book, title of the book, and page or pages.

6. J. J. Rousseau, "The Social Contract," in Sebastian Jensen, *Documents Illustrative of the Eighteenth Century,* pp. 14-21.

If the document is unsigned, begin with its title.

G. A very similar citation covers the case of one book quoted in another. Suppose you are reading William Smith, *The Decline of Peru.* In a footnote Smith mentions a book by Roger Culpepper, *The Last of the Incas,* and includes a quotation from it. Part of this quotation you wish to put in your paper. You have not read Culpepper; only the foonote in Smith referring to Culpepper. The citation is as follows:

7. Roger Culpepper, *The Last of the Incas,* p. 93, cited in William Smith, *The Decline of Peru,* p. 265.

H. References to newspapers give the title of the paper, date of issue, and page, if the place of publication is included in the title; otherwise the city is given in parenthesis after the title.

8. *Chicago Tribune,* July 14, 1937, 14.
9. *Our Sunday Visitor,* (Huntington, Indiana) May 3, 1955, 6.

Note that the titles of books, magazines, and newspapers are always underlined (they would be italicized in print. Titles of chapters or articles *in* books, magazines, or newspapers are, however, placed in quotation marks.

I. When a reference is made to a source already cited in a footnote it is often convenient to use various Latin abbreviations in place of repeating a lengthy book title or description of a magazine or encyclopedia article. The commonest such abbreviations are *op. cit., loc. cit.,* and *ibid.* They are always underlined.

10. J. W. Wilson, *op. cit.,* I, 134.
11. Richard K. Morris, *loc. cit.,* 177.
12. *Ibid.,* 180.

Note carefully the differences above. *Ibid.* is used only when the reference is to the source cited in the footnote *immediately preceding. Ibid.* means that everything is the same as in the preceding footnote except the page. *Op. cit.* is used when the reference is to a *book* cited in a previous footnote but *not* in the footnote immediately preceding (in this case Wilson's book was cited in footnote 2 but not in footnote 9). *Loc. cit.* is used in exactly the same may as *op. cit.* save that *loc. cit.* applies to newspapers and periodicals and *op. cit.* to books.

BIBLIOGRAPHY

The bibliography is a list of all the books, articles, and other sources of information that have been of value in preparing the essay. It is not necessary to cite a footnote from a source in order to include that source in the bibliography. However, the source should have at least added to one's knowledge of the problem in order to be included. Textbooks should not be included in the bibliography since it is assumed that a student reads his textbook. If accurate and full information has been taken down on the note cards the bibliography can be prepared from them. The bibliography is always located at the end of the essay. The bibliography page is numbered.

In printed books or lengthy dissertations the bibliography is usually broken down into several categories. For a short research paper it is sufficient to divide it into primary and secondary sources. A primary source is normally any account or document contemporary with the events described and written by someone in a position to know the facts. A secondary source is a general history or other account *based* on primary sources or other secondary accounts, but not contemporary with the event described. There is one exception to this general distinction. For recent history (within the last century) an account is considered primary only if it was written by an actual participant in the events described or by one who was in a position to observe them at first hand. An account written by someone who lived at the same time but had no such first hand knowledge would be regarded as secondary.

Each category, primary and secondary, should be arranged alphabetically, according to the author's *last name*. (Note the difference from footnote form, where the author's first name comes first.) If the name of the author is not known list the item alphabetically according to the first significant word in the title. Each bibliographical item should contain, in that order, author or editor, complete title, edition (if there has been more than one), place of publication and publisher (except for newspapers, magazines, and encyclopedias), and date of publication.

Following are samples of bibliographical entries. Note the form and punctuation. The item should be entered exactly like this.

Primary Material

Blaine, James G., *Twenty Years in Congress,* 2 vols. Norwich, Connecticut:
     Henry Holt and Co., 1884, Vol. I.
Chicago Tribune, July 14, 1937.

Note that if the item extends to more than one line the second
and all succeeding lines are indented five spaces. (Just the opposite
of paragraphs or footnote indentation.) The purpose of this is to
enable the reader to glance quickly down the left side of the bibliography page and see the chief sources of information.

Note also the item from Blaine. As it appears here, the entry indicates that Blaine's work *totals* two volumes and that the writer
has used the first volume. Had he used both volumes "Vol. I"
would have been omitted and the entry would have ended with
"1884." The inference would have been clear that both volumes
had been used. The number of volumes in *the whole set* is always
shown immediately after the title of a book, and the volume or
volumes *you used* after the date of publication.

Secondary Material

"Black Death," *Encyclopaedia Britannica,* (11th ed.), III, 550-554.
Jones, George. *History of Rome.* New York: Macmillan and Co., 1945.
Morris, Richard K. "Taxation in Medieval France," *American Historical
     Review,* XXVI (1927), 173-195.
Wilson, J. W. *Life of Julius Caesar.* 3 vols. Chicago: Henry Regnery and
     Co., 1956.

Note in examples one and three (above) that the page numbers
for the *entire article* are included. In the case of books written by
one person page numbers are never included. If the book is a cooperative work like the *Cambridge Modern History* include the page
numbers for the particular chapter read: e.g.,

Macdonald, J. R. Moreton. "The Terror," Chapter XII, *The Cambridge
     Modern History,* VIII, 330-361.

INDEX

101 Devotions
for His
Princesses

Carolyn Larsen

christian
art gifts®

Holly & Hope: 101 Devotions for His Princesses

© 2015 Christian Art Gifts Inc., IL, USA
Christian Art Kids, an imprint of Christian Art Publishers, RSA

Designed by Christian Art Kids

Images used under license from Shutterstock.com

Scripture quotations are taken from the *Holy Bible*,
New Living Translation. Copyright © 1996, 2004, 2007, 2013
by Tyndale House Foundation. Used by permission of Tyndale
House Publishers, Carol Stream, Illinois 60188.
All rights reserved.

Scripture quotations are taken from the *Holy Bible*,
Contemporary English Version®.
Copyright © 1995 by American Bible Society.
All rights reserved.

Printed in China

ISBN 978-1-4321-2389-5

20 21 22 23 24 25 26 27 28 29 – 17 16 15 14 13 12 11 10 9 8

Printed in Shenzhen, China
July 2020
Print Run: 100818

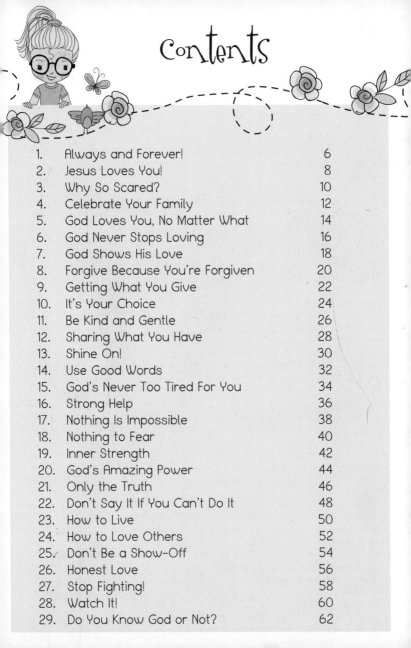

Contents

Always and Forever!

Do you wonder if God really does love you? How can He when you are sometimes mean to your friends? What about when you lose your temper or talk back to your mom? Does He love you anyway?

He does! God loves you no matter what — always and forever! And, even better, He wants to help you learn to do better all the time. So, ask Him for His help! He will give it!

*The faithful love
of the LORD never ends!
His mercies never cease.*

Lamentations 3:22

7

Jesus Loves You!

Do you know the Bible verse John 3:16? It's a famous verse that says that God loves the whole world. But, do you believe that He loves you personally? Do you sometimes wonder if Jesus would have died if you were the only one who needed to be saved?

Well, wonder no more! Jesus came to earth and lived and died for ... YOU! He loves you that much! He would have done it all just for you!

"*God loved the people of this world so much that He gave His only Son, so that everyone who has faith in Him will have eternal life and never really die.*"

John 3:16

9

Why So Scared?

Yikes! First day in a new school in a new town. That's scary, huh? That would make you feel scared and all alone.

Guess what? God understands that you get scared sometimes. Tell Him you're scared and He will help you. He will remind you how much He loves you. He will remind you that He is with you. So, ask Him to help you be brave!

3

The LORD *your*
God is living among you.
He is a mighty Savior.
He will take delight in you
with gladness. With His love,
He will calm all your fears.
He will rejoice over
you with joyful songs.

Zephaniah 3:17

11

Celebrate Your Family

You love your family, but be honest ... sometimes your brother or sister can be a pain. Sometimes your parents have too many rules.

Did you know that your parents love you to the moon and back? Families are a good example of how much God loves you. In fact, He says you are His child! He is your Father and yes, He loves you to the moon and beyond!

Think how much the Father loves us. He loves us so much that He lets us be called His children, as we truly are.

1 John 3:1

13

5

God Loves You, No Matter What

Imagine how people feel when a storm hits and their homes are flooded. Families lose everything – clothes, furniture, toys and even pets. They might be tempted to think God has stopped loving them.

He hasn't. It's important to remember that nothing can take God's love away. Problems don't mean He has stopped loving us. Trouble doesn't mean God has stopped loving us. In fact, He is sad when you're hurting and He wants to help you through your problems.

*Nothing in all creation
can separate us from
God's love for us
in Christ Jesus our Lord!*

Romans 8:39

15

God Never Stops Loving

Not everything in life is forever. Pets run away. Friends move away. Nothing is forever ... except one thing!

God's love! Nothing can take it away from you. He will never stop loving you. He is always with you. He will always take care of you. He is with you when you have problems. He helps you in any way you need. You can depend on God's love for you.

I am like an
olive tree, thriving in
the house of God.
I will always trust
in God's unfailing love.

Psalm 52:8

17

God Shows His Love

Do you sometimes wonder if God really loves little old you? Well, look around. No doubt you can see proof of God's love for you. Where? How about in …

- Our beautiful world
- The sun
- The moon and stars
- Your family
- Your friends
- Your home
- Your food and clothing.

God IS love and He shows His love to you in many ways, every single day!

We know how much
God loves us, and we have
put our trust in His love.
God is love, and all who live
in love live in God,
and God lives in them.

1 John 4:16

19

Forgive Because You're Forgiven

Your friend may say something that hurts your feelings. She may not play fair in a game. Of course you will feel hurt about those things. Who wouldn't? But, when your friend says she's sorry, do you forgive her right away?

You know, everyone messes up sometimes so you should forgive your friend. It's the right thing to do. Make peace with your friends and forgive them just as God always forgives you.

Be kind and merciful,
and forgive others,
just as God forgave
you because of Christ.

Ephesians 4:32

21

Getting What You Give

Would you like people to be kind?
Then you be kind.
Would you like people to be fair?
Then you be fair.
Would you like people to be helpful?
Then you be helpful.

God says that to get others to treat you the way you want to be treated, you have to start the ball rolling by treating them that way first. You will get back what you give out.

"Treat others as you want them to treat you."

Matthew 7:12

23

It's Your Choice

There's a saying, "The ball is in your court."
It means that sometimes your words or
actions decide what happens next.

Let's say someone says something
mean to you or treats you badly.
If you explode with shouts and accusations,
then a fight will happen. But, if you respond
gently and kindly, you might keep a fight from
starting. It's how God says to treat others ...
with kindness.

A kind answer soothes
angry feelings, but harsh
words stir them up.

Proverbs 15:1

25

11

Be Kind and Gentle

You have accepted Jesus as your Savior. You are God's child. What does that mean? Are you any different from those who don't know God?

You should be! You should speak with kindness and not say mean things about others. You should play fair and treat others with respect. By acting like this you are treating others the way a child of God should.

26

God loves you
and has chosen you
as His own special people.
So be gentle, kind,
humble, meek, and patient.

Colossians 3:12

Sharing What You Have

When you are hungry, you need food. When you are cold, you need a jacket. When you go to school you need a backpack. If you have all the things you need, then thank God and your parents! What about kids who don't have what they need? If you have two of something, could you give one to someone else? That's what God says to do — help one another.

If we have all we need
and see one of our own people
in need, we must have pity
on that person, or else
we cannot say we love God.

1 John 3:17

29

13

Shine On!

Why is it important for your actions to show that you obey God and the teachings in the Bible? Is it so that people will think you are awesome? Nope. It's important because it shows people what God is like.

If you love others and treat them with kindness, it shows God's love. If you are generous and helpful, it shows God's love. If you are humble and gentle, it shows God's love.

"Let your good deeds
shine out for all to see,
so that everyone will praise
your heavenly Father."

Matthew 5:16

31

14

Use Good Words

Words are so important. Your words can make a friend sad. They can make her feel bad about herself. They can make her think she isn't loved. They can make her feel that even God doesn't love her. Be careful of your words. Use words that make your friend feel good about herself. Words that help her know she is special to you and to God!

Don't use foul or abusive language. Let everything you say be good and helpful, so that your words will be an encouragement to those who hear them.

Ephesians 4:29

33

15

God's Never Too Tired For You

"Mom, will you play with me?" Have you ever asked that only to have Mom reply, "I'm too tired right now." Your parents work hard at their jobs and clean, cook, do laundry and yard work. They get tired. When people get tired it's sometimes hard to pay attention to others. That never happens with God though. He never gets tired. He is always ready to take care of you.

Have you never heard?
Have you never understood?
The LORD is the everlasting God,
the Creator of all the earth.
He never grows weak or weary.
No one can measure the depths
of His understanding.

Isaiah 40:28

35

16

Strong Help

Trouble comes. Maybe a grandparent passes away or your dad loses his job. It might be that your best friend gets really mad at you or that you get in big trouble with your parents. Whatever it is, you can be sure that trouble will come. What do you do when you have trouble? Turn to God. He is strong and powerful and He is always ready to help you get through your troubles.

God is our refuge and strength,
always ready to help in times of trouble.

Psalm 46:1

17

Nothing Is Impossible

Sara's mom is sick. People tell her to pray and ask God to help her mom get well. But her mom just keeps getting worse. Sara wonders if she is so sick that God can't help her. If Sara understood this verse in Matthew she would know that she can pray for anything because nothing is too hard for God. He wants you to ask Him for what you want.

Jesus looked straight
at them and said,
"There are some things that
people cannot do,
but God can do anything."

Matthew 19:26

39

18

Nothing to Fear

Sometimes you feel like you don't have any friends. You feel alone. That's not a very good way to feel. It's kind of scary. But, you aren't really alone because God is always with you. He's your friend. You just need to remember that He will give you strength to get through the lonely times. Just ask Him!

"Don't be afraid,
for I am with you.
Don't be discouraged, for I am
your God. I will strengthen
you and help you. I will hold
you up with My
victorious right hand."

Isaiah 41:10

41

19

Inner Strength

"I can't." Have you ever felt that you can't do something? "I can't go to a new school. I don't know if I can make a new friend. I don't think I can pass this test." Some things in life are scary so how can you do them? You need strength that only comes from God helping you, so ask Him for His help. He will give it. He promises.

*I can do everything
through Christ,
who gives me strength.*

Philippians 4:13

43

20

God's Amazing Power

God's power is amazing. You may not even think about some of the most powerful things He does every day. He makes the sun come up. He makes the wind blow. He makes the ocean waves go only so far. He sends the sun to bed each night and brings the moon and stars. Day in and day out He does this work. You can count on your powerful God for whatever you need.

"Did you ever tell the sun to rise?
And did it obey? Did it take hold
of the earth and shake out the
wicked like dust from a rug?"

Job 38:12–13

45

21

Only the Truth

"Mandy flunked the math test. She has never passed a math test," Heidi told everyone. Well, guess what? That is a big, fat lie. Heidi doesn't know what Mandy's grade was. She's just trying to make Mandy look dumb. Telling lies is just not nice.

A God-follower tries to be honest. So, do not tell lies about anyone else. Do not lie about yourself. Be honest. That's the way to honor God.

An honest witness does not lie;
a false witness breathes lies.

Proverbs 14:5

47

22

Don't Say It
If You Can't Do It

One of your friends told you that you are her best friend, but she doesn't act like it. She told lies about you. She chose to play with others and left you by yourself. There was nothing in her actions that backed up her claim to love you.

It doesn't fool anybody, especially not God, if you say you love someone but then are unkind to them. Mean what you say or don't say it.

Dear children, let's not
merely say that we love
each other; let us show
the truth by our actions.

1 John 3:18

23

How to Live

"I want to live the way God wants, but I'm not sure how." Have you ever said that? Well, just in case you ever wonder how you're supposed to treat other people, read Galatians 5:22-23.

It's simple: Love others. Be joyful. Be peaceful. Show patience, kindness, goodness. Be a faithful friend to others and to God. Be gentle. Don't lose control of your temper.

The Holy Spirit produces this
kind of fruit in our lives: love, joy,
peace, patience, kindness, goodness,
faithfulness, gentleness, and self-control.
There is no law against these things!

Galatians 5:22-23

51

24

How to Love Others

Love others. That's simple, right? But the middle part of this command makes it a little tougher. Jesus says to love others the same way He loves you. What does that mean? He gave up everything for you. He left heaven and came to earth. He died and rose again ... because He loves you. Can you love others that much? What would that look like?

"Now I am giving
you a new commandment:
Love each other. Just as
I have loved you, you should
love each other."

John 13:34

25

Don't Be a Show-off

No one likes a show-off.
Do you know someone who
brags about herself? Maybe
about what a great soccer
player or musician she is.
Does she ignore the fact that
others are good at things, too?

Humility is the God way —
not bragging but lifting others
up so they feel recognized
and important. You can't lift
someone else up if you're
bragging about yourself!

*Don't be selfish;
don't try to impress others.
Be humble, thinking of others
as better than yourselves.
Don't look out only for your
own interests, but take an
interest in others, too.*

Philippians 2:3-4

55

26

Honest Love

When you hear about people who don't have enough food to eat or warm clothes to wear or even a place to sleep, how do you feel? Do you think, "Oh well."

Or, do you want to help them? If you want to do something — GOOD FOR YOU! That's what God says real love looks like.

God says to help each other and do what you can for people who need stuff just to survive.

Suppose you see
a brother or sister who has
no food or clothing, and you say,
"Good-bye and have a good day;
stay warm and eat well" —
but then you don't give that
person any food or clothing.
What good does that do?

James 2:15-16

27

Stop Fighting!

How do you stop a fight that is starting? What do you do when a friend is going on and on about something and you want to snap right back with reasons why YOU are right and she is wrong? You just stop. Stop talking. Stop arguing. Stop defending yourself. Just stop. Because love is what stops fights. Say something kind. Say something loving and unexpected. That's what will stop the fight. You can do it!

Hatred stirs up trouble;
love overlooks the
wrongs that others do.
Proverbs 10:12

Watch It!

"I'm so mad at you! I'm not your friend anymore!" Has anyone ever said something like that to you? Or maybe you've said it to someone.

Whoa. Saying angry words like that can get you into big trouble. God says to keep your anger under control and to be careful not to call anyone a bad name just because you're mad. Be careful to treat others with respect — even when you're mad!

*Don't get so angry
that you sin.
Don't go to bed angry.*

Ephesians 4:26

61

29

Do You Know God or Not?

Annie goes to church with her family every week. She learns Bible verses for Sunday school quizzes. Her Bible lies on her nightstand. She prays. If you asked Annie she would say, "Of course I'm a Christian." You might say you are, too. But the truth comes out in how you treat others. Are you kind, gentle, honest, encouraging? In other words do you show love to others? That's what shows you are a Christian.

Dear friends,
let us continue to love
one another, for love
comes from God.
Anyone who loves is a
child of God and knows
God. But anyone who
does not love does not
know God, for God is love.

1 John 4:7-8

63

30

Go the Extra Mile

Here's a story about love ... Brooke doesn't have any friends. She is mean to everyone. But, Cori feels bad for Brooke so, she asks to sit by Brooke at lunch and to hang out with her sometimes. At first Brooke is super mean to Cori, but eventually she sees Cori's love for her — even though she shows no love for Cori. Soon they are friends and Brooke starts being nicer to everyone!

"If you love only those
people who love you,
will God reward you for that?
Even tax collectors
love their friends."

Matthew 5:46

31

Trust the One Who Knows

Sometimes it's so hard to know the right thing to do. Sometimes you don't understand what is going on. Some of your friends tell you one thing and others tell you something else. Whew. It can get confusing. The smart way to know the best thing to do is to go to God. Trust Him to help you know what to do and when to do it. Just ask Him for help and He will give it!

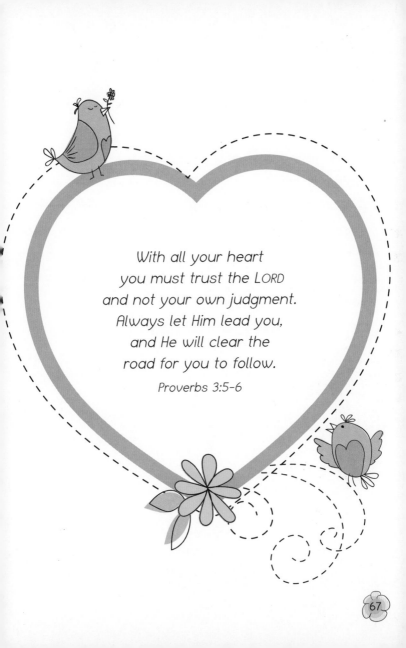

With all your heart
you must trust the LORD
and not your own judgment.
Always let Him lead you,
and He will clear the
road for you to follow.

Proverbs 3:5-6

32

Jesus Never Changes

Change is not easy. Unfortunately life is made up of changes. People move away. Friends leave. Teachers change. Does all the change scare you sometimes? But there is one thing … one Person … who never changes. Jesus promises to love you, no matter what. He is always with you. He takes care of you. Jesus never changes. You can count on it.

*Jesus Christ
is the same yesterday,
today, and forever.*

Hebrews 13:8

33

Good Sleep

It's nighttime. You should be
sleeping but you're not because
you're scared. You think there are
monsters in the closet or under the bed.
You'd like to run into your parents'
room but you try to be brave.
One thing that will help you to be brave is to
remember that God is taking care of you.
He is standing watch over you and
protecting you. So, lie down and sleep.
Let God stand guard!

You, LORD, are the light
that keeps me safe.
I am not afraid of anyone.
You protect me,
and I have no fears.

Psalm 27:1

71

34

What Is Faith?

Do you believe in God? If you've gone to church your whole life you've probably heard "have faith in God" dozens of times. You think, "Okay." But what does it mean? What is faith? Faith is believing that what the Bible says is true — even if it seems impossible, even if you don't understand it, even if you can't see how it might work. Just believing because the Bible says it's true.

*Faith makes us sure
of what we hope for and gives
us proof of what we cannot see.*

Hebrews 11:1

Look for the Good

Does God promise that your life will be wonderful and happy and problem free since you know Him? No, it doesn't work like that. Problems will still come along. But, God promises to teach you to trust Him, depend on Him and believe that He loves you — no matter what problems you have. God is bigger than your problems.

We know that God
is always at work for the good
of everyone who loves Him.
They are the ones God
has chosen for His purpose.

Romans 8:28

75

36

A Sweet Promise

God promises good things for you. Then why do you have problems and make bad choices? Why do you get in trouble? Because you learn the most when you have problems. When you are scared, worried or in trouble, you turn to God for help. When He helps you learn to trust Him. He wants you to grow into a beautiful young woman so don't dread your problems, learn from them.

"I know the plans I have for you," says the LORD. "They are plans for good and not for disaster, to give you a future and a hope."

Jeremiah 29:11

77

37

Don't Give Up

Do you try to obey your parents and God but keep messing up? And after a while you decide it's just too hard to live for God so you don't try anymore? Other people have felt the same way before but they made it, so, what should you do? Ask God for help! Keep turning to Jesus and learn from Him. It takes a whole lifetime to learn to live for Jesus, so don't give up!

We must get rid of everything that slows us down, especially the sin that just won't let go.
And we must be determined to run the race that is ahead of us.

Hebrews 12:1

38

A Thankful Heart

Take a minute and think about your prayers.
Do most of your prayers start with,
"Do this" or "Help this" or "Can I have"?
If most of your prayers are asking God
to do something for you, then you're like
most people. Here's a good reminder to take
time to thank God for everything in your
life — good things AND hard things.
Be thankful for the difficult things because
you will learn good lessons from them.

Be thankful in all
circumstances,
for this is God's will
for you who
belong to Christ Jesus.
1 Thessalonians 5:18

39

Give Up Worrying

Worry takes a lot of energy.
When you're worried about something,
it's pretty much all you can think about.
No matter what else is happening, the thing
you are worried about is always on your
mind. What can you do about it? Pray.
Simple answer but the very best thing you
can do. Tell God what you're worried about.
Ask Him to handle it. He will. He loves you.

Don't worry about anything;
instead, pray about everything.
Tell God what you need,
and thank Him for all He has done.

Philippians 4:6

83

40

Pleasing Words

Do your words honor God and show respect for Him? It's okay to be honest with Him about your fears and worries and even your disappointments. But be careful that in your prayers and your thoughts, you show the respect He deserves. Remember that you are even allowed to speak to Him — the Creator of everything — because He loves you and cares about you very much. Let that respect show in the words you speak.

*Let my words and my thoughts
be pleasing to You, LORD,
because You
are my mighty rock
and my protector.*

Psalm 19:14

85

41

Taking Care of Others

"I want to pray for my friends who have problems. But, I don't know what to tell God to do." Have you ever felt that way?

Here's the cool thing — you don't have to tell God what to do. His Spirit is in your heart and He knows what you should pray.

All you need to do is bring your friend before God and the Spirit will guide your prayers. How cool is that?

*Pray in the Spirit
at all times and on
every occasion.
Stay alert and be
persistent in your prayers for all
believers everywhere.*

Ephesians 6:18

42

Keep on Praying

Do you get discouraged? Don't stop praying!
Do you feel sad? Don't stop praying! Are you
worried? Don't stop praying! Are you scared?
Don't stop praying! Are things going great?
Don't stop praying! Are you super happy?
Don't stop praying! Are you feeling blessed
beyond belief? Don't stop praying! You get
the idea. No matter what is going on in your
life — happy stuff, hard stuff, sad stuff, joyful
stuff — keep on praying!

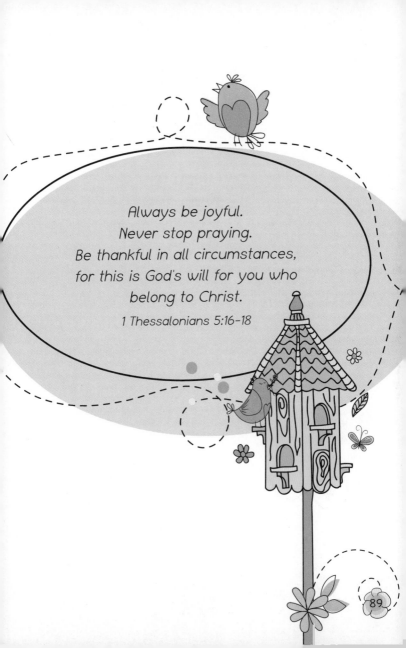

Always be joyful.
Never stop praying.
Be thankful in all circumstances,
for this is God's will for you who
belong to Christ.

1 Thessalonians 5:16–18

43

Just Ask!

Decisions can be tough. Maybe there are some decisions you need to make, like if you're going to be mean to someone because your friends are or if you're going to trust God in hard times. Those kinds of decisions are hard because you don't want your friends to be mad at you, but you want to serve God. So ... what do you do? Ask God! He will give you wisdom and be glad you asked!

If any of you need wisdom, you should ask God, and it will be given to you. God is generous and won't correct you for asking.

James 1:5

91

44

Supporting One Another

If you have a friend who has some pretty serious problems you may wish that you could help her. But there may not seem to be any way that you can. Well, there is one way you can help. You can pray! God promises that honest prayer from a heart that wants the right things makes a difference. God not only pays attention to those prayers, He answers them!

*If you have sinned,
you should tell each other what
you have done. Then you can
pray for one another and
be healed. The prayer
of an innocent person is
powerful, and it can
help a lot.*

James 5:16

45

I Don't Know What to Pray

Let's be honest. Sometimes it is hard to know what to ask God for. When your dad needs a job but the one he gets is in another state, how do you pray? When someone you love gets sick, how do you pray? The answer is not to skip praying altogether. It's to trust God's Holy Spirit to help you. He knows what to ask for. He will pray for you.

In certain ways we are weak, but the Spirit is here to help us. For example, when we don't know what to pray for, the Spirit prays for us in ways that cannot be put into words.

Romans 8:26

95

46

Ask the Right Things!

Can you really ask God for whatever you want and He will give it to you? Sort of. It's important to stay close to Jesus and know the Bible. If you do this it will mean that you are asking God for things that He really wants to give you. Your motivations will be right. You will be asking for things that honor and glorify God. Stay close to Jesus. Know the Bible.

"But if you remain in Me
and My words remain in you,
you may ask for anything you want,
and it will be granted!"

John 15:7

97

47

Patient Prayer

Are you a patient girl? When you ask for something do you want it RIGHT NOW or are you okay with waiting? Do you get impatient with Mom and Dad when they don't do things as quickly as you want? Do you even get impatient with God? Do you believe that God hears your prayers and can you wait for Him to answer when He is ready? If you can — you truly trust Him!

I waited patiently
for the LORD to help me,
and He turned to me
and heard my cry.

Psalm 40:1

99

48

Simple Prayer

Some can say prayers that are fancy, beautiful prayers. How about you? Does it make you nervous to pray aloud? It certainly is nice that some people can pray aloud like that. But your prayers aren't for other people to admire. They are spoken to God from your heart. Don't worry about fancy words. Just tell God how you're feeling and what you're worried about. That will be good enough.

"When you pray,
don't babble on and on
as people of other religions do.
They think their prayers are
answered merely by
repeating their words again
and again."

Matthew 6:7

49

Talking to God

Prayer is a private conversation with God. You don't need to have the conversation in front of others. Sometimes it needs to be private so you can honestly tell God what's on your mind and what you want Him to do.

Make sure you have private prayer time just as you have private talks with a best friend. Private and honest conversation with God is talking to the One who loves you more than anyone else does!

"When you pray,
go away by yourself,
shut the door behind you,
and pray to your Father
in private. Then your Father,
who sees everything,
will reward you."

Matthew 6:6

others can Pray for You, Too

It is important to have private prayer time where you can honestly tell God what's on your heart.

It is also important to share prayer requests with other people so they can pray for you, too. There is power in numbers. As others join you in prayer, you are reminded that you aren't alone and that others care. It doesn't hurt to have a lot of people on your team!

"I also tell you this:
If two of you agree here on earth
concerning anything you ask,
My Father in heaven will do it for you."

Matthew 18:19

51

Praise God!

It's easy for your prayer time to get swallowed up with asking God for things you want Him to do for you.

But there is another kind of prayer that is really important — praise. Prayers of praise tell God that you know how awesome and powerful He is.

Prayers of praise are also good for you because you stop and realize His power and strength, His love and care.

Let everything
that breathes sing
praises to the LORD!

Psalm 150:6

52

It All comes from God

What are you thankful for? Your family? God gave them to you. Your home? God gave it to you. Your friends? They are a gift from God. The beauty of nature? God made it all. Animals? Thunderstorms? Snow? Books? Music? Whatever it is — IT CAME FROM GOD!

Tell Him how awesome He is. Tell Him how thankful you are!

*Every good and perfect
gift comes down from
the Father who created all the
lights in the heavens. He is always
the same and never makes
dark shadows by changing.*

James 1:17

53

God's Faithful Love

Knowing you are loved is the best! The people who love you want good things for you. They celebrate with you when great things happen for you.

They will help you as much as they can.

Knowing you are loved by the most awesome God is even better. God loves you and nothing will take His love away. It's good to be reminded of His love. Accept His love and thank Him for it.

*Give thanks to the LORD,
for He is good!
His faithful love endures forever.*

Psalm 136:1

54

What Did You Say?

"I love you, God! You're so awesome!"
"My parents are so mean. I wish I had a different family!"

Whoa, two different kinds of words spoken here — by the same mouth! One set of words praises God. The other sentence complains about one of God's precious gifts. These kinds of things should not be spoken by a person who says she loves God. Watch your words. Keep them positive and thankful and not critical or complaining.

My dear friends,
with our tongues we speak
both praises and curses.
We praise our Lord and Father,
and we curse people who
were created to be like God,
and this isn't right.

James 3:10

113

55

My Strength Comes from God!

Sometimes you get discouraged. Sometimes you feel lonely. Sometimes you feel sad. Sometimes you face something that you do not think you can handle. You feel that you're being asked to do things that you just aren't strong enough to do. All of that is okay. Do you know why? Because God is strong enough for whatever you face. His strength is your strength.

Just ask Him to help you and He will!

The LORD is my strength,
the reason for my song,
because He has saved me.
I praise and honor the LORD —
He is my God.

Exodus 15:2

56

Shout It from the Mountaintop!

How wonderful it is to praise God! It's joyful to tell Him how you appreciate all the things He does for you. It's good to name specific things you love — from ocean waves to rainbows to friends to family. Praise God for it all.

But don't stop there. Don't just tell God — tell others, too! That may be how some of your friends first learn about God's amazing love and power. Shout His praises from the mountaintops!

*Sing to Him; yes,
sing His praises.
Tell everyone about His
wonderful deeds.*

1 Chronicles 16:9

57

Singing a New Song

When Jesus comes into your life, He changes things. He gives you hope for the future. He gives you strength. He answers your prayers. He loves you!

The joy of the Lord puts a new song in your heart and it is a song of praise to God! Other people will learn about Him and His love through your joy! Celebrate His love!

You gave me a new song,
a song of praise to You.
Many will see this, and they
will honor and trust You,
the LORD God.

Psalm 40:3

58

One Day Everyone Will Praise God!

Some people won't have anything to do with God. They don't think that He is very important. These people don't give Him credit for all He does; all He makes; all He gives. They refuse to praise Him. But one day they will.

The Bible says that EVERYONE will praise God one day. Everyone will bow to Him and worship Him. Don't wait for someday — praise God now!

God says, "Everyone will kneel
down and praise My name!"

Romans 14:11

121

59

Everyone Needs Help

Why should you be thankful for Jesus' death and resurrection? Because Jesus died to pay for your sins. If He hadn't done that, you couldn't have a friendship with God. You could never hope to be in His heaven someday.

Every person who has ever lived; every person alive right now; every person who ever will live is a sinner. Jesus made it possible for you to know God.

For everyone
has sinned;
we all fall short
of God's glorious
standard.

Romans 3:23

Jesus Paid for Your Sin

The Bible tells us that we are all sinners. Not one of us is without sin. Sin separates us from God.

A price must be paid for sin. Jesus paid that debt for you. The only Person who never sinned paid the price for all the people who do sin. That's a lot of love — and that love is for you.

*Sin pays off with death.
But God's gift is eternal life given
by Jesus Christ our Lord.*

Romans 6:23

125

61

Not Me!

"I'm not a sinner. I've never stolen anything. I've never committed a crime. I am kind and honest and helpful." Is that how you feel about yourself? Do you compare yourself to others and think that you're not so bad?

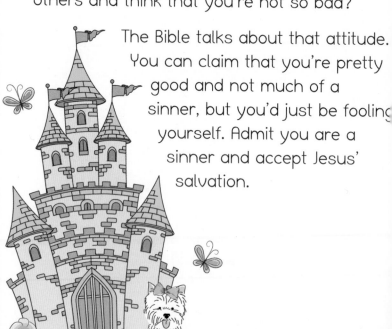

The Bible talks about that attitude. You can claim that you're pretty good and not much of a sinner, but you'd just be fooling yourself. Admit you are a sinner and accept Jesus' salvation.

*If we claim we have no sin,
we are only fooling ourselves
and not living in the truth.*

1 John 1:8

62

The Next Step

First you must admit that you are a sinner. You need Jesus' gift of salvation. The next step is repentance. That means that you say you're sorry for sinning and will turn away from it. Repenting means you will try not to do it anymore.

Of course, you can't do that without God's help and strength. Ask Him to help you and He will.

*Repent of your
sins and turn to God,
so that your sins may
be wiped away.*

Acts 3:19

63

One Way

There is only one way to get to heaven. Only one. That is by believing in Jesus and accepting Him as your Savior.

Some people will try to tell you that it's good enough to be a nice person. Some might try to tell you that there are other ways or that God wouldn't really keep people out of heaven. That's not what the Bible teaches. Jesus is the only way.

Only Jesus has the power to save! His name is the only one in all the world that can save anyone.

Acts 4:12

131

64

It's a Gift

The privilege of knowing God is a gift. The promise of being in His heaven someday is a gift. It's all a gift that Jesus gives because He loves you so much. No one can do anything to earn salvation. No one can brag that they did this or that and made it happen. Salvation is possible only because of God's amazing love.

You were saved by faith in God, who treats us much better than we deserve.

This is God's gift to you, and not anything you have done on your own. It isn't something you have earned, so there is nothing you can brag about.

Ephesians 2:8–9

133

65

Keep Going!

If you try to stop doing wrong things by yourself, you will get really tired. If you try to be strong when life gets really hard, you'll get really tired.

Without God's strength helping you through life, you will just get worn out. But, if you ask for God's help, His strength will fill you with power and you will be able to keep going and going.

Even young people
get tired, then stumble
and fall. But those who trust the
LORD will find new strength. They
will be strong like eagles soaring
upward on wings; they will walk
and run without getting tired.

Isaiah 40:30–31

66

Give It to God

There's a new girl at school. Some girls pick on her. You're a Christian. You want to show God's love to her but you don't want the others to get mad and pick on you, too. What do you do?

Tell God the whole thing — about the new girl, the mean girls, and not wanting them to pick on you. Ask for His help. Trust Him. He will help you do the right thing.

Do what the LORD wants, and He will give you your heart's desire. Let the LORD lead you and trust Him to help.

Psalm 37:4–5

137

67

You Make a Difference

Hamsters run on a little exercise wheel. They run and run but they don't get anywhere. Sometimes life feels like that. There may be a girl who is very unfriendly to you. But you try to be nice anyway. She is still mean. You go out of your way to do nice things. She's still mean. It feels like nothing you do makes a difference. Don't get discouraged. What you do for God will make a difference.

*My dear friends, stand
firm and don't be shaken.
Always keep busy working for
the Lord. You know
that everything you do for Him is
worthwhile.*

1 Corinthians 15:58

139

stuff Isn't Important

Do you always want the latest stuff and nag your parents for things that you see others have?

We must watch out that we don't become selfish and want, want, want.

We must think of others who have less than us and try to help them.

People are more important than things.

The Bible says money mustn't be our master.

"You cannot be the slave of two masters. You will like one more than the other or be more loyal to one than to the other. You cannot serve God and money."

Luke 16:13

69

Sticking With God

Living for God means being humble. That means you don't brag about how great you are. You give God credit for helping you be kind and loving. You openly thank Him for His gifts to you. You praise and honor Him. You fight the urge to brag and take credit — that urge comes from the devil anyway.

So, resist it and the devil will run away as you stick closer to God.

So humble
yourselves before God.
Resist the devil,
and he will flee
from you.

James 4:7

143

70

LiVe like This

God makes it easy for you to know how to live for Him. Let's look at what this verse says:

1. Do what is right — be honest, fair, considerate and caring to others.

2. Love mercy — show forgiveness and kindness to others, even if they aren't sorry for the things they do.

3. Be humble — don't try to take credit for what God has given you or done for you. Give Him the credit!

*O people, the LORD has told
you what is good, and this
is what He requires of you:
to do what is right,
to love mercy, and to walk
humbly with your God.*

Micah 6:8

145

71

Follow the Leader

Figuring out how to live in new situations can be scary. Situations such as when your parents split up or when someone you love dies. Maybe there are other scary things you have to deal with. Whatever it is — don't be scared. Just follow your Leader.

God will go ahead of you and prepare the way for you. Stick close to your Leader and trust Him to help you.

Be brave and strong!
Don't be afraid.
The LORD your God will
always be at your side,
and He will never abandon you.

Deuteronomy 31:6

72

God Holds Your Hand

Remember when you were a little girl going somewhere with your mom. As you came to a street, did your mom tell you to stop? Did she take your hand and hold it as you crossed the street together? Did you feel safer with Mom holding your hand? Look at this verse — God holds your hand, too. He is right beside you no matter what you are going through. You're never alone!

"I am the LORD your God.
I am holding your hand,
so don't be afraid.
I am here to help you."

Isaiah 41:13

149

73

Healthy Stuff

You know that if you eat healthy foods then your body is healthy and strong. What you put in your body plays a big part in how strong and healthy you are.

It's the same with your heart. If you read God's Word and learn what it teaches, you are putting healthy thoughts in your heart so it will be strong and healthy. Then you will be filled with love and power and you will be strong.

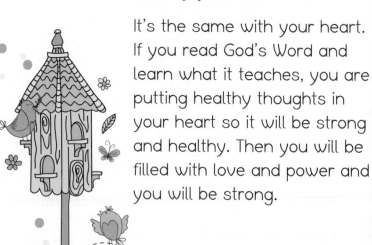

God's Spirit doesn't make
cowards out of us.
The Spirit gives us power,
love, and self-control.

2 Timothy 1:7

151

74

Real Peace

Do you have trouble sleeping when you're nervous or scared about something? Does your mind create all kinds of scenes of how bad things could happen to you? There is no peace in your heart or life when you're worried or scared.

But, if you can get your heart to trust God to take care of whatever is worrying you, then you will find real peace.

God is always there to help us and He gives us peace in our hearts when we trust Him.

You will keep in perfect peace all who trust in You, all whose thoughts are fixed on You!

Isaiah 26:3

153

75

Love Letters

Do you like to get mail? Getting cards or letters from people who live far away is a sweet reminder that they are thinking about you.

Did you know that God has a letter for you, too? His Word — the Bible — is filled with stories and reminders of how much He loves you. Read it, let the love fill your heart and you will learn to love Him more and more.

Let the message about
Christ completely fill your lives,
while you use all your wisdom to
teach and instruct each other.
With thankful hearts,
sing psalms, hymns, and spiritual
songs to God.

Colossians 3:16

76

Putting Action to Your Words

Some people say they love God but their actions don't match up with what they say. Their actions are unkind. They say mean things and gossip about others.

A person's true love for God shows in her actions because she keeps His commandments to be kind and love others. How do you know what those commandments are? They are found in the Bible. Read it to learn how God wants you to live.

*Loving God means
keeping His commandments,
and His commandments
are not burdensome.*

1 John 5:3

157

Put the Light On

When you go into a dark room and don't turn on a light you step on stuff left on the floor. That hurts! A light would have shown you the way and helped you to avoid the stuff on the floor.

God's Word is a light for you. When you read it and learn from it, it becomes a guide for you to know how to live. It helps you to avoid things that would hurt you.

Your word is a lamp to guide my feet and a light for my path.

Psalm 119:105

159

A Secret Weapon

You will be tempted with stuff for your whole life. Things like the urge to say unkind things or to be selfish.

Sometimes you might be tempted to join friends in a dishonest or dangerous activity. How do you fight these temptations? By having God's Word in your heart to remind you of how important it is to obey Him. Knowing God's Word gives you strength! It's like a secret weapon against temptation.

I have hidden Your word in my heart, that I might not sin against You.

Psalm 119:11

161

79

Your Instruction Book

Learning how to do something new is exciting but it's always a good idea to know the instructions for how to do things. It makes the learning process go faster.

You have an "Instruction Book" for how to live for God — the Bible! God gave you the instructions in it so you can learn to love and trust Him. It teaches you to love others and to do what is right.

Everything in the Scriptures is God's Word. All of it is useful for teaching and helping people and for correcting them and showing them how to live.

2 Timothy 3:16

163

80

Choose to Obey

You have a choice. When selfish or mean thoughts come into your mind, you can choose to replace them with nicer thoughts. If you choose to stick with the mean thoughts they will eventually become actions — things you do.

Memorize God's Word and let what it teaches become your choices. Push away the bad thoughts and replace them with God's Word.

Get rid of all the filth
and evil in your lives,
and humbly accept the word God
has planted in your hearts,
for it has the power to
save your souls.

James 1:21

81

Forever!

Can you think of things that will last forever?
Houses?
Mountains?
Oceans?
People?
Some of those things will last a long time but none of them will actually last forever. One thing that will last forever is God's Word. He says that is true. So, no matter how many people ignore God or say He isn't important, His Word will never disappear. It will always be important to know and obey God's Word.

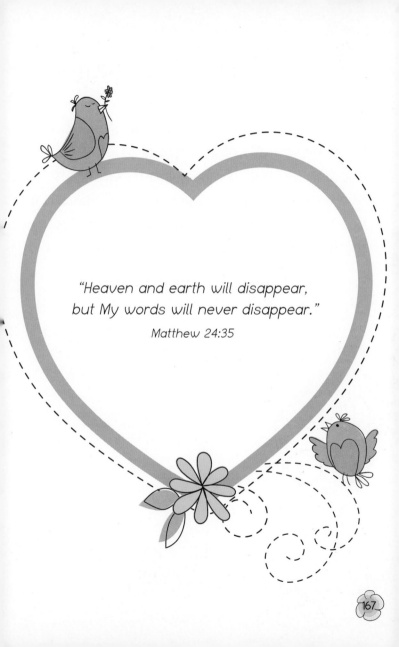

"Heaven and earth will disappear,
but My words will never disappear."

Matthew 24:35

82

No Secret Thoughts

Your thoughts are private, right? You can think selfish or unkind thoughts. No one knows. You can think loving thoughts. No one knows every thought you think. This idea is not true — God knows every thought you think.

So, God knows if you are thinking kind or unkind thoughts. You know it, too. Let God's Word guide your thoughts and teach you how to live.

What God has said
isn't only alive and active!
It is sharper than any double-edged
sword. His word can cut through our
spirits and souls and through our joints
and marrow, until it discovers the desires and
thoughts of our hearts.

Hebrews 4:12

83

Important Food

It's no fun to be hungry. When your tummy starts yelping for food you want to eat right away!

Jesus knew that food is important for you. But He also made a point that there is an important food for your soul. It's God's Word. Reading and learning God's Word helps you know how to obey God and how to live peacefully and kindly with others.

It's food for your soul!

But Jesus told him,
"No! The Scriptures say,
'People do not live by bread alone,
but by every word that comes
from the mouth of God.'"

Matthew 4:4

171

84

Good Things

What are you thinking about? Who do you spend time with? It matters. It's difficult to live for God if you are spending time with and listening to the advice of people who don't care about Him. They will pull you away from Him. It is better to spend time with those who are also obeying God.

You can learn together to live for Him and to know His Word and keep it in your heart.

God blesses those people
who refuse evil advice and won't follow
sinners or join in sneering at God.
Instead, the Law of the LORD makes them happy,
and they think about it day and night.

Psalm 1:1-2

173

85

Obey Your Parents

Is it easy for you to obey your parents or do you have trouble with that? Everyone has trouble obeying sometimes. There are even times when grown-ups don't feel like obeying. But, it's important to obey your parents. Why? Because their rules are to keep you safe. Some are to help you learn how to be kind and respectful of others.

Obeying your parents pleases God and helps you learn to be a better person.

Children, always obey your parents, for this pleases the Lord.

Colossians 3:20

175

86

Show Kindness

It's nice to be forgiven when you hurt someone, isn't it? But, are you willing to forgive someone who hurts you? The way to live for God and get along with others is to understand that your friends or family do not always mean to hurt you. So be willing to forgive them. Remember that God forgives you over and over so doing that for others is the way God wants you to live.

Put up with each other,
and forgive anyone who
does you wrong, just as
Christ has forgiven you.

Colossians 3:13

The Golden Rule

Treat others the way you would like them to treat you. If you want others to be kind, you be kind to them. If you want others to forgive, you forgive. If you want people to be caring, you care. If you want people to be fair, you be fair.

They may not treat you these ways immediately, but eventually they notice how you are treating them, and even if they don't, you can feel good about how you are treating others.

The Golden Rule:

_"Do to others as you
would like them to do to you."_

Luke 6:31

88

Start Now

Some kids say, "Oh, I'm just a kid so it doesn't matter whether I try to live for God. I'll worry about that when I'm a grown-up." Well, that's not how God feels about it. He says that even as a young girl, how you behave is noticed. It's a good idea to start the pattern of living for God while you're young. Others will notice and that could turn their thoughts to living for God, too.

*Even children
are known by the way
they act, whether their
conduct is pure,
and whether it is right.*

Proverbs 20:11

89

Jesus Loves children

Do you know that Jesus spent time with children? Sometimes it might seem that grown-ups are very busy and that they don't have time for you.

But Jesus always has time for you. You can pray to Him any time of the day or night and He hears you.

Take time to speak to Him right now!

Jesus said, "Let the children come to Me. Don't stop them! For the Kingdom of Heaven belongs to those who are like these children."

Matthew 19:14

183

90

We Need God

Have you ever said something like, "I try to obey God but it's hard. I'm not strong enough. I can't do it." Sounds like discouraged words, doesn't it? But getting to that point of giving up control is actually a good place. It means that you know that YOU can't obey God by yourself. You need His help. His power in your life is strongest when you understand how much you need it.

"My kindness is all you need. My power is strongest when you are weak." So if Christ keeps giving me His power, I will gladly brag about how weak I am.

2 Corinthians 12:9

185

91

Work Hard!

"Time for chores!" Mom calls on Saturday morning. What's your response? Do you grumble and complain? Do you try to get out of doing your chores? Do you rush through your chores and not do them very well? That shouldn't be your attitude.

You should work hard without complaining because that shows honor to God and your parents. Imagine that God Himself says it's time for chores and that He is watching how you do your work.

Work willingly at
whatever you do,
as though you were
working for the Lord
rather than for people.

Colossians 3:23

187

92

Love Matters

Does it matter whether you are nice to other people? Even more than nice, is it important that you love others? It sure is. Jesus said you must love God completely — as much as you can. But He didn't stop there. He said it is just as important to love your neighbor ... not just a little bit but as much as you love yourself! Wow.

Ask Jesus to help you to love Him with all your heart and to love others.

Jesus replied,
"The most important
commandment is this:
'The LORD our God is the one
and only LORD. And you must
love the LORD your God with
all your heart, all your soul,
all your mind, and all your
strength.'" Then He said,
"'Love your neighbor
as yourself.' No other
commandment is
greater than these."

Mark 12:29-31

189

93

Don't Turn Away

There are people who have less than you do. Maybe you know of places where there has been a flood or a storm and the people who live there were left with very little.

The Bible says that real love for others means helping them by sharing what you have. When you know of people who need help, don't turn away. Help in any way you can. That is showing love.

Most important of all,
continue to show deep love
for each other, for love covers
a multitude of sins. Cheerfully
share your home with those who
need a meal or a place to stay.

1 Peter 4:8-9

94

Good Friends

What makes a good friend? A friend is loyal - she stands up for you no matter what. You can tell a good friend anything and you know that she won't tell anyone else.

A good friend will help you when you need help, cry with you, laugh with you and celebrate with you. If you have a friend like this, thank God. If you are a friend like this to someone else, thank God!

*A friend is always loyal,
and a brother is born
to help in time of need.*

Proverbs 17:17

95

All Fun & Games?

Do you think that Romans 8:28 means that you will never have problems? No, it doesn't mean that. Do you know why? It's because sometimes you learn the most important lessons when you have to work through problems. The more you have to depend on God and trust Him, the more you learn about His strength and power. So God brings good things out of problems.

Life isn't all fun and games, but Jesus is always with us, through the good and the bad.

We know that God
causes everything to work
together for the good of
those who love God and
are called according to His
purpose for them.

Romans 8:28

195

96

Turn the other cheek

When someone hurts you, do you want to get even? That's a natural reaction, but it isn't the way God says to react. He says to turn the other cheek, that is, forgive them. Jesus said this in the middle of His teaching about loving your enemies.

The most important thing is to show God's love to others — sometimes that means doing something very hard.

"I tell you not to try to get even with a person who has done something to you. When someone slaps your right cheek, turn and let that person slap your other cheek."

Matthew 5:39

97

Love Your Enemies

Jesus says to love your enemies. Not only love them, but pray for them! Does He mean pray that they will get what's coming to them? No. Does He mean pray that their teeth fall out? No. He means pray that they will come to know Him as Savior. Pray for good things in their lives.

If you pray for good things for someone it's hard to be angry with them. It might be difficult to pray for someone you don't like, but ask God to help you.

"But I say,
love your enemies!
Pray for those who
persecute you!"

Matthew 5:44

199

98

Would You Do It for Jesus?

If you could, would you give Jesus some cold water on a hot day? Would you visit Him when you knew He was lonely? Jesus says when you do those kinds of things for others, it's like doing them for Him. It's important to be kind to others and to show them what Jesus' love and concern looks like by how you treat them. Then, it's like doing those things for Jesus.

The King will answer,
"Whenever you did it for any
of My people, no matter
how unimportant they seemed,
you did it for Me."

Matthew 25:40

99

Someday Is Now!

Maybe you love Jesus a lot right now. Maybe you think, "Someday when I'm a grown-up, I will work hard for Jesus. I'll tell others about Him. I will do whatever work He has for me. Someday I will serve Him." You don't have to be a grown-up to serve God. You can live for Him now and others — especially others who are your age — will see His love through the way you live!

Don't let anyone
think less of you
because you are
young. Be an example
to all believers in what
you say, in the way
you live, in your love,
your faith,
and your purity.

1 Timothy 4:12

100

Real Love Defined

The chapter of 1 Corinthians 13 describes what God's love looks like. This is the kind of love God wants you to have for others. Once you read this definition you know that this love is not at all selfish. The love God gives wants the very best for the person you love and so any selfishness or anger just melts away as you love them.

Love is kind and patient,
never jealous, boastful, proud, or rude.
Love isn't selfish or quick tempered.
It doesn't keep a record of wrongs that
others do. Love rejoices in the truth,
but not in evil.

1 Corinthians 13:4–6

101

Put On Love

The Bible says often that it is very important to love God and love others. It just isn't possible to say that you love God but then not love other people. It wouldn't be honest. And your love can't be only for your friends.

Love is what ties people together so that when one person hurts, another person helps. And when one person succeeds, another person celebrates. Love is the most important.

*Love is more important
than anything else.
It is what ties everything
completely together.*

Colossians 3:14

Carolyn Larsen is an author, actress, and an experienced speaker with a God-given passion for ministering to women and children. She has spoken at conferences and retreats around the United States, Canada, and India. Carolyn has written over 40 books for children and adults. Her writing has won various awards. Carolyn lives in Glen Ellyn, Illinois, with her husband, Eric. They have three children and are proud grandparents.